This book is dedicated to the staff of NewSpring Church. You are the most amazing people in the world! Thank you for allowing me to be a leader who is learning as I go. Thank you for allowing me to make mistakes. Thank you for allowing me to be real. And thank you for all the amazing work you do each and every week. We've come so far . . . and the best is yet to come.

CONTENTS

FOREWORD

ALL MY LIFE, IT'S BEEN MY GOAL TO ADD VALUE TO PEOPLE. For almost forty years, the primary way I've done that is by communicating about leadership. It is my passion because I believe that everything rises and falls on leadership.

When you help a person become a better leader, you help all the people that leader impacts. There are few things more rewarding than seeing leaders changed by being challenged, inspired, and equipped to grow, and then seeing them make a positive impact in their companies, churches, families, and communities.

Two decades ago, I taught leadership primarily in church environments. At that time, one of my personal goals was to help one thousand pastors to grow their churches beyond one thousand people in weekly attendance.

In 1999, after teaching a conference targeted at helping pastors to reach this milestone, I received a letter from a young man who informed me that he was planting a church, and he wanted me to know that he desired to be one of the pastors who would one day reach a thousand. He told me that he'd listened to my leadership lessons on tape, read my books, and felt as if my teaching had set him up to be successful. That young pastor's name was Perry Noble.

In the fall of 2002, I received another letter from Perry. He wanted me to know that his church had broken the one-thousand barrier in attendance, and he graciously thanked me for being influential in his life.

What a rewarding moment that was. Having the opportunity to add value and help a leader in some small way is the reason I write books, host conferences, and speak at events.

Imagine my surprise when less than a year later I received another letter from Perry. This time he let me know that his church had reached two thousand. And he again expressed gratitude for all the leadership resources my company and I had created, which were helping him to grow.

Five months after that, I received another letter. His church attendance had reached three thousand people.

At this point I asked my assistant, Linda, to write this young man to let him know I had read the letters, was proud of him, and would love to have lunch with him sometime. He must have called Linda the same day, because it wasn't long before I saw a lunch appointment with him on my calendar.

When I arrived for lunch, Perry was waiting for me, pen and notebook in hand. Oftentimes when I meet with young leaders, they talk a lot about themselves and try to impress me with their knowledge and achievements. That wasn't the case with Perry. Instead, he impressed me with his *questions*. For two and a half hours, he picked my brain.

That day, I mostly tried to give him the benefit of my experience and the lessons I'd learned from my mistakes. But I also gave him a couple of assignments and told him I would be happy to have lunch with him again sometime.

A month later, Perry e-mailed Linda with a description of what I had asked him to do, what he had done, and the results he had seen. And there was a request for another lunch.

I have no idea how many times I've met with Perry over the last decade, but every time I do, I'm rewarded by hearing about his follow-through—and seeing the growth of his church. (He still writes me to say thank you every time he reaches another one thousand people. And he recently texted me to say that sixty thousand people attended his church one weekend!)

But what's most remarkable is that as Perry and his church have grown, his hunger to learn has actually increased. And so has his desire to help people and add value to them.

Perry has been an exceptional student and practitioner of leadership. And that's why I'm delighted to present this book to you. Everything I know about leadership I've learned from the Bible. The same is true for Perry, so everything he teaches in this book is rock solid and highly practical. Perry's reading of 1 Corinthians 13 and his application of it to leadership is insightful, encouraging, and heartfelt. It will help you become a better leader. And that will help you fulfill God's calling on your life, because everything rises and falls on leadership.

So turn the page. You're going to enjoy this journey.

John C. Maxwell

BEFORE YOU READ THIS BOOK, *PLEASE* READ THIS

I'M A BIBLE GUY. I'm a pastor. I'm a leader.

But I didn't start out that way. In fact, quite the opposite: in high school, I was voted least likely to succeed. With my extreme procrastination, my habit of doing the least amount of work possible, and my lack of commitment, I was the guy who made the top half of my class possible.

My leadership journey began in 1991, when I was hired to be a part-time youth pastor at a small church in Pickens, South Carolina. I had no idea what I was doing, no idea how leadership worked. Then, the weekend before my first day, both the senior pastor and the music director resigned . . . which left me as the only staff member in the entire church the first Sunday I was there.

Talk about being thrown into the fire!

But looking back now, I can see how much I learned in that church.

I learned that the best leaders don't have titles, but they do have a voice people want to listen to.

I learned that different people respond to different styles of leadership and that what works for one person doesn't work for all.

I learned that there's a difference between great leadership and control or manipulation.

There was one Sunday in particular when these lessons started to come into focus for me.

I'd been asked to teach the senior men's Sunday school class, which was comprised of men sixty-five and up. I wasn't very popular with these guys; after all, I was the young buck who was allegedly trying to change everything in "their" church.

My first response to this request was "No, thank you." However, it wasn't long before I found out this wasn't actually a request.

I was assured that this would be a piece of cake. There was a Sunday school lesson book, and all I had to do was show up, teach the lesson, pray, and then leave.

All week leading up to my first teaching session, I put off preparing for the class; after all, if I just had to read the book, I figured I'd have zero challenges.

On Saturday night, I finally forced myself to sit down with the study book, and when I turned to the date of the lesson I was supposed to teach, I nearly went into cardiac arrest.

The title of the lesson was "Sex"!

I was barely nineteen years old, and I had the responsibility of teaching a group of senior adult men about sex.

I prayed for God to take my life! What in the world would I say to a group of men who had forgotten more about sex than I even knew?

I couldn't have known at the time that this event would serve as a turning point for me in my leadership at the church.

That Sunday morning, I walked into class, opened with a prayer, and told them I noticed the lesson I was supposed to teach was about sex. With a laugh, I said, "I'm sure there's nothing I can teach you guys about sex, and I'm not even going to try!"

They laughed, and I continued.

"What I would like is for you guys to tell me a little bit about you, how you came to Christ, and how you began attending this church."

There were about eight or nine men in the class, and I listened to their stories and paid attention to what they had to say. After that "sex talk" with the senior-adult men in the church, their opinion of me did a 180. They no longer saw me as the young rebel trying to ruin what they'd worked so hard for, and I no longer saw them as the old men who were unwilling to change.

Leadership isn't about lecturing people—it's about listening to them, understanding where they're coming from, and showing that you care.

After a few years in Pickens, I was offered a job at a church that was about two miles from the college I was attending. I was there for more than six years, during which time I served as the youth pastor, the children's pastor, the college pastor, and the worship pastor, plus a few other titles. I described myself as the "minister of miscellaneous."

But tension in this church existed between the senior adults and me. (Anyone see a pattern here?) They were convinced I was trying to hijack their church, and I was convinced they were stuck in their ways.

The senior pastor came to me one day and told me that something had come up in his schedule, and he wouldn't be able to drive a group of senior adults to their "senior-adult convention" at the beach. He needed me to drive them (six hours one way) and make sure they were taken care of.

Talk about Daniel in the lions' den!

I told him I didn't want to.

He said I didn't have a choice.

I told him that was not in my job description.

He told me to please go back and read the sentence that said, "Other duties as assigned by the senior pastor."

So I did it . . . and it turned out to be one of the best leadership experiences of my life.

The first hour of the drive was intense because, as I said, these people were not too fond of me. However, over time, the walls between us started to come down. We began having meaningful conversations, and a level of understanding was established.

By the end of the trip, these senior adults were some of my best friends at the church. They formed what I secretly referred to as the senior-adult mafia and refused to let any other senior adult bad-mouth me.

In my time at that church, I learned that the only way I could become a great leader was by submitting to the leadership I was serving under.

I learned that leaders aren't those who make declarations but rather those who are willing to serve others and do whatever it takes to turn a vision into a reality.

I learned that if I'm the smartest person in the room, then I'm in the wrong room, because I need to constantly surround myself with people who are smarter than I am.

In the fall of 1999, I founded NewSpring Church. We started with fifteen people in a living room, no employees, no budget. But we did have a vision to create a church that would reach people far from God and teach them how to follow Jesus step-by-step.

Today we have nineteen campuses across the state of South Carolina, and we reach an average of thirty-five thousand people each weekend. Our organization operates on a $50 million budget with more than four hundred staff members.

So why has the church taken off like this?

I believe it has a lot to do with leadership—not necessarily my leadership, but the leadership of those around me and the lessons I've learned from other leaders along the way.

My reason for sharing this is not to boast. I'm not one of those natural leaders who was the high school class president or who rose to the top of his graduating class in college. I took remedial classes in grade school and made a 790 on my SAT. Almost everything I've learned about leadership has come through firsthand experience—with some successes but even more failures.

The principles in this book aren't just theory for me; they aren't ideas I came up with and then wrote down but haven't actually done. They've all been tested in the fires of real life, with real people. I believe these truths are timeless, and they work for anyone in any situation. More than that, I believe they will change you, as well as whatever group of people you happen to lead.

When people talk about leadership, they often use words like *vision*, *boldness*, and *influence*. But I think the heart of great leadership lies elsewhere. The most excellent way to lead has nothing to do with the number of followers you have on social media or how big your office is or how much money you get paid. True leadership is about living for something greater than yourself.

And the place I've learned the most about leadership is from a source that might surprise you: a Bible chapter that you're more likely to hear at a wedding than in a conference room.[1]

I should give a warning right from the beginning: the most excellent way to lead is also the most difficult. It goes against our

---

[1] If you aren't a Christian or if you have problems with sections of the Bible, let me say right up front that I'm honored you would read this book. I use a lot of biblical examples on these pages, and my hope is that by the end, you'll understand the Bible a little more clearly and see that this book points to Jesus, the greatest Leader of all time. (Think about it: He never even wrote a book, traveled more than one hundred miles from His hometown, led an army, or ran for public office, yet today there have been more books written about Him and more art done in His name than any other person in history.)

natural tendencies and the culture we live in, and it highlights the fact that leadership is ultimately not about the leader. However, this upside-down model of leadership isn't just biblical; it's also the most effective and most rewarding way to lead.

Whether you're an entrepreneur, a receptionist, a midlevel manager, or a new parent, I hope this book will encourage you to see every opportunity in life as a chance to lead in the most excellent way.

SUMMARY STATEMENTS

→ The best leaders don't have titles, but they do have a voice people want to listen to.

→ The most excellent way to lead is also the most difficult.

→ Leaders aren't those who make declarations but rather those who are willing to serve others.

→ Leaders do whatever it takes to turn a vision into a reality.

#BestWayToLead

CHAPTER 1

WHAT DOES IT MEAN TO BE A LEADER?

I LOVE TO SHAG, and if you've ever done it, I'm sure you love it too.

I once hired a guy onto our staff who had moved to South Carolina from the northeastern part of the United States.

During one of our early conversations, he was trying to figure out more about the area, and he asked me what people in our community do for fun.

I told him that a lot of people like going to the lake, hiking, fishing, or playing golf. But then I said something that caused him to look at me like someone had punched him in the throat: "And a lot of people around here love to go out in groups and shag."

Silence—dead silence.

My new employee looked at me like I had lost my dang mind.

So I felt the need to continue to explain how awesome shagging is.

"A lot of people in our church shag."

His jaw dropped.

"I'm not that good of a shagger myself," I continued, "but my wife took shagging lessons in college, and she's really good at it."

At this point he thought he'd agreed to work for one of the most perverted pastors in the country!

I should let you know that in South Carolina, our state tree is the palmetto, our state bird is the Carolina wren . . . and our state dance is called the shag, which after my conversation with my new staff member, I learned means something different in other parts of the world.

This exchange with my staff member reminded me of something a friend had told me years ago: "Words don't have meanings; people have meanings." So when we say certain words or phrases, they may mean something completely different to the person we're talking to than they do to us.

Based on my twenty-five years as a leader, I think there's no word more often misunderstood than *leadership*.

That's not because there's a lack of information. New books come out on the topic every year, and new blog posts pop up every day. I recently came across an article from CNN about the qualities that make a good leader. The article featured input from various leadership experts, and it's amazing how many different opinions are out there. The list included twenty-three attributes, some of which included confidence, vision, and influence.

Let's take a look at the following three viewpoints on leadership, just for starters.

I have a hunch many people would agree that leadership equals confidence, and I think there's some truth to that.

A leader has to be able to make tough decisions.

A leader has to be willing to go against popular opinion.

However, while confidence is important, I don't believe it's the most excellent way to lead.

Joseph Stalin was confident. He made tough decisions. But because his confidence was self-centered and cruel, millions of people lost their lives. Or consider Pharaoh, the leader of Egypt who was so stubbornly confident about his own power that he allowed his people to suffer under ten plagues (see Exodus 7–11). He was confident, but he certainly wasn't great.

People may also argue that leadership equals vision—and again, I believe that's true to a certain extent.

Leaders have to be able to focus on a task with a laser-like intensity to avoid getting distracted by things of lesser importance. And not only do they have to have a clear vision themselves but they also have to be able to communicate that vision to the team.

The trouble is that visionary leadership apart from the proper focus can result in disaster. Adolf Hitler was a visionary. He had a clear plan, and he refused to allow anything to distract him from carrying it out. However, since his goal was rooted in evil and self-centeredness, the world experienced one of the worst atrocities in history—the Holocaust.

In Jesus' day, the religious leaders, the Pharisees, had a very focused vision. The problem was that they were so worried about their own legalistic rules and their positions of power that they made an enemy out of Jesus, the Messiah they were supposed to be waiting for.

Some people think that true leaders simply have the gift of influence.

When people think of leaders, they look for the people who walk into a room and have what I call the "it factor"—the ability to get a group of people to catch their vision and follow them. If leaders don't have influence, then they won't be effective long term.

A leader has to be able to produce passion in people and compel them to action.

A leader has to be able to unify a group of people who may not have much in common besides the goal they're trying to achieve.

However, while I believe influence is essential for leadership, I don't think it's the best way to lead.

Bernie Madoff had influence—so much that he was able to convince thousands of people to invest in his Ponzi scheme to the tune of $65 billion. Until his world came crashing down in 2008, he was one of the most respected financial experts in the world. He was highly influential, but I have a hunch no one today would call him a great leader.

So if great leadership is not defined by confidence, vision, and influence, as most of the world would say, then what is the most excellent way to lead?

It's simple: the most excellent way is leadership by love.

A COUNTERCULTURAL STYLE OF LEADERSHIP

Hold on—don't throw this book across the room. I know this sounds countercultural and maybe even a little touchy-feely, but I promise I won't ask you to sit in a yoga pose around a campfire while you share your deepest feelings with your team.

This isn't just some idea I came up with one night after eating a Meat Lover's pizza with extra cheese and having a weird dream. The place I get this idea from is the Bible. More specifically, from a guy named Paul, who wrote most of the New Testament.

Paul was an excellent leader. He started at least fourteen churches (possibly more) at a time when the church was less popular than it is today. In Paul's day, church wasn't merely a social gathering but a place where people who followed Christ came together, knowing it could cost them their lives if they were caught doing so.

If you've ever started a business or a ministry or any kind of organized group, you know the challenges associated with building something from the ground up. And there was Paul, starting churches all over the Mediterranean rim with no technology, no leadership books, and no apps on his smartphone.

One of the churches Paul founded was in a place called Corinth. He wrote letters to the church there, and we have two of them recorded in the New Testament: 1 Corinthians and 2 Corinthians. In 1 Corinthians 12, the emphasis of Paul's writing to the church is on spiritual gifts, leadership, and the importance of working together. In 1 Corinthians 14, he continues this line of reasoning as he encourages leaders to sound a clear call for their followers.

But right in the middle of these two chapters we find 1 Corinthians 13. It's a short section (just thirteen verses), tucked between these two leadership chapters. At first glance, these words seem to be more like advice for newlyweds than instructions for the conference room. The thirteenth chapter of 1 Corinthians is, after all, commonly known as the "love chapter," and if you've ever attended a Christian wedding ceremony, you've likely heard a verse or two quoted from it.

For years, the placement of this chapter puzzled me.

It seemed like Paul was writing about leadership, and then he paused and thought, *Hmm, maybe I should write something Christians can use in their wedding ceremonies one day!* After he penned 1 Corinthians 13, he picked up the subject of leadership again and continued to talk about it in chapter 14.

But the Bible wasn't originally separated by chapters and verses (those were added later to help people find certain Scripture passages). Once I had that realization, it hit me like a brick in the face: 1 Corinthians 13 is primarily a chapter on how to lead, not how to have a great marriage.

In 1 Corinthians 12:31, Paul says, "I will show you the most excellent way."

The most excellent way to what?

To be a great person?

To be a great spouse?

To be a great date?

I don't believe so. Paul is continuing his discussion about leadership here, and when he says he's going to show you the most excellent way, I believe he's saying, "I will show you the most excellent way to lead."

I guarantee that the principles from 1 Corinthians 13 will help you become a better leader.

It doesn't matter if you're a single mother trying to lead your family, a student organizing a group of people to fight for a cause, an entrepreneur trying to get a start-up off the ground, a pastor trying to lead your church, or a CEO leading a business—if we practice leadership by love, we will become leaders other people actually want to follow.

Let's take a look at the first few verses from this chapter through the lens of leadership:

> If I speak in the tongues of men or of angels, *but do not have love*, I am only a resounding gong or a clanging cymbal. If I have the gift of prophecy and can fathom all mysteries and all knowledge, and if I have a faith that can move mountains, *but do not have love*, I am nothing. If I give all I possess to the poor and give over my body to hardship that I may boast, *but do not have love*, I gain nothing.

1 CORINTHIANS 13:1-3 (EMPHASIS ADDED)

Make no mistake about it: loving others is a really big deal—not just in personal relationships but also any time there is a leader-follower relationship. Most people think love should be left out of the workplace and other leadership settings, but as this passage shows . . . love is more important than casting great vision, being extremely intelligent, or even working hard for a cause.

The way we look at other people is important—and when we see them through the lens of love, our capacity to lead significantly increases.

LEARNING FROM THE BEST

Jesus was the most excellent leader who ever lived. He was once asked which of the commandments was the most important, and this was His response:

> "Love the Lord your God with all your heart and with all your soul and with all your mind." This is the first and greatest commandment. And the second is like it: "Love your neighbor as yourself." All the Law and the Prophets hang on these two commandments.
>
> MATTHEW 22:37-40

"Love God; love others," He said—and notice that He didn't separate the two. If we want to be excellent leaders, then loving other people is not optional. It isn't something we do only on the days it comes naturally or when we feel like it.

Loving people isn't easy.

People will hurt you.

They will disappoint you.

They will turn on you.

They will gossip about you.

They will fight you.

Leadership by love doesn't sound sexy on the surface, but it's the most effective—and most rewarding—way to lead in the long term.

When it comes down to it, people don't need a flashy leader who can quote inspirational lines or has the most carefully constructed vision statement or has the charisma to charm a bunch of followers. They need someone who cares enough about them to come alongside them and help them become the best version of themselves they can be.

They need someone who guides them with patience and kindness, without insecurity or vanity. They need someone who helps them climb higher through grace and honesty, who takes bullets for mistakes, who gives the benefit of the doubt. They need someone who offers hope when others won't, who perseveres when others don't. In short, they need a leader who loves.

Those who lead through love don't just change the culture they're in; they change the world.

SUMMARY STATEMENTS

→ The most excellent way to lead is leadership by love.

→ If we practice leadership by love, we will become leaders other people actually want to follow.

→ Loving others is a big deal—not just in personal relationships but also anytime there is a leader-follower relationship.

→ Love is more important than casting great vision, being extremely intelligent, or even working hard for a cause.

#BestWayToLead

CHAPTER 2

PATIENT

Love is patient.

I CORINTHIANS 13:4

IF THERE WERE AN AWARD given for Most Impatient Person of the Year, I would win it every time.

If I'm in a grocery store and there are two lines, I'll get in one line but mentally hold my place in the other. And if I see that I would have gotten through the other line first, it will ruin the rest of my day.

If I'm driving down the road and someone pulls out in front of me and then proceeds to go so slowly that the seasons actually change as we're cruising down the road, I have to admit that ungodly thoughts rush through my mind.

Patience is not one of those virtues that come naturally to me, and having talked to other leaders, I don't think I'm alone in this. Since most leaders are driven, goal-oriented types, it makes sense that many of us don't like to wait for what seem like unnecessary delays.

Patience isn't something most of us are born with, and it doesn't come automatically the moment we get a new title or take on a leadership position. However, the good news is that patience can be developed over time.

Let me fill you in on a little secret though: we don't become patient when things are easy; we tend to learn patience through storms in life.

People who say they've never cussed have never had to deal with a car seat.

If you've ever put a car seat into a car, then you understand where I'm coming from here. The first time I tried to put one in for our daughter, it took about five minutes for me to lose it. I was sweating, crammed into the back of my car, and wishing for the good old days when car seats weren't around.

However, my wife reminded me that the purpose of the car seat wasn't my comfort but the protection of our daughter. My patience with the process just might result in saving the life of our little girl.

All too often, leaders give in to the temptation of impatience, and they utterly lose it. They begin yelling, throwing things, and making what I call "anger assertions" (e.g., "I'm going to fire everyone in here if you all don't shape up.").

But even leaders who aren't so vocal can struggle with impatience. Maybe they're not volcanoes, spewing verbal lava on everyone in their paths, but they are on a slow boil on the inside. They become extremely judgmental and refuse to trust people who "just don't get it."

This type of quick-tempered leadership does work—temporarily. However, an impatient leader will eventually become an ineffective leader, since people don't want to work for a person who may snap at any moment just because things aren't going their way.

The first thing Paul said about leadership through love is that "love is patient" (1 Corinthians 13:4). I believe there are two areas we must learn to be patient in: the process and the people.

BE PATIENT WITH THE PROCESS

As leaders, we often get an idea and want to attack it with the tenacity of a pit bull.

We want results; we want to see things happen—we want *progress*. This can have an incredibly good side when it comes to getting things done, but if we aren't careful, we'll wind up leaving dead bodies in our wake.

There's no true progress for the leader who is unwilling to patiently embrace the process.

One of the greatest leaders in the Old Testament is David. When we first meet him in the Bible, he isn't some powerful leader of a multimillion-dollar organization; rather, he's a shepherd, which was considered a lower-level, blue-collar job in his day. He was the youngest in his family, and no one had a reason to see any sort of potential in him.

However, even though he came from nothing, David became one of the greatest leaders of all time. This didn't happen overnight, though.

The first time we meet David is in 1 Samuel 16, when he was anointed king over Israel sometime in his late teens. But as David learned, there's always a gap between anointing and appointing.

Can you imagine knowing as a teenager that you're going to be the king of a nation?

What would you do?

What decisions would you make?

How would you expect people to respond to you?

When it comes to leadership, people often want the position, but they won't take the posture that causes them to become a great leader— patiently dealing with the people and situations immediately in front of them.

In the years between David's anointing and when he actually took the throne, he didn't try to rush God's plan, boast in his gifting, or take matters into his own hands to get his predecessor, Saul, out of office. Instead, he embraced the process and did whatever he was asked to do—and he did it well.

After David was anointed king, he wasn't immediately rushed to the palace; instead, he had an opportunity to take a job with King Saul as something of a part-time musician. We see this story unfold in 1 Samuel 16:18-23:

> One of the servants answered, "I have seen a son of Jesse of Bethlehem who knows how to play the lyre. He is a brave man and a warrior. He speaks well and is a fine-looking man. And the LORD is with him."
>
> Then Saul sent messengers to Jesse and said, "Send me your son David, who is with the sheep." So Jesse took a donkey loaded with bread, a skin of wine and a young goat and sent them with his son David to Saul.
>
> David came to Saul and entered his service. Saul liked him very much, and David became one of his armor-bearers. Then Saul sent word to Jesse, saying, "Allow David to remain in my service, for I am pleased with him."
>
> Whenever the spirit from God came on Saul, David would take up his lyre and play. Then relief would come to Saul; he would feel better, and the evil spirit would leave him.

What I find fascinating about this story is that when David was given the opportunity to serve the current king in this capacity, he didn't hold up his hand and say, "Oh, I'm sorry, you must be mistaken. You see, I'm anointed. I'm special. I'm a snowflake—there's no one else like me, so you're going to have to find something more important for me to do."

He patiently embraced the process—and the process put him in a position to succeed.

David is probably most famous for defeating Goliath. Even if you're not familiar with the Bible, you've most likely heard the story of this kid with a slingshot who took down a giant who made Shaquille O'Neal look small.

Let's take a look at 1 Samuel 17:12-20:

Now David was the son of an Ephrathite named Jesse, who was from Bethlehem in Judah. Jesse had eight sons, and in Saul's time he was very old. Jesse's three oldest sons had followed Saul to the war: The firstborn was Eliab; the second, Abinadab; and the third, Shammah. David was the youngest. The three oldest followed Saul, but David went back and forth from Saul to tend his father's sheep at Bethlehem.

For forty days the Philistine came forward every morning and evening and took his stand.

Now Jesse said to his son David, "Take this ephah of roasted grain and these ten loaves of bread for your brothers and hurry to their camp. Take along these ten cheeses to the commander of their unit. See how your brothers are and bring back some assurance from them. They are with Saul and all the men of Israel in the Valley of Elah, fighting against the Philistines."

Early in the morning David left the flock in the care of a shepherd, loaded up and set out, as Jesse had directed. He reached the camp as the army was going out to its battle positions, shouting the war cry.

Every leader wants to have experiences like this one—overcoming huge obstacles, experiencing a win when odds indicated a sure loss, doing what others claimed couldn't be done.

However, some of David's best leadership training happened not on the battlefield but in the less dramatic moments when he waited on God's timing. As he played his harp for the king, he was an excellent steward of what was right in front of him.

David didn't allow the news that he'd be king one day to go to his head. Instead of lording it over his older brothers and the rest of his community, he patiently embraced his responsibilities of taking care of the family's sheep.

When people are new in leadership, they're often tempted to bypass what they consider the smaller things so they can step into the bigger and better tasks of their new roles. However, if a person can't be trusted with the little things, why would they think they could be trusted with much? God often uses those experiences that seem inconsequential to us as the training ground to prepare us for the job ahead.

I can honestly say if I hadn't learned what it was like to lead a small team of five volunteers, there's no way I would have been prepared to lead a staff of more than four hundred people.

We also see David's humility when his dad asked him to take his brothers and their commanders some food (see 1 Samuel 17:17-18). He could have said, "Oh, Father, you poor old man, don't you know who I am? I've been anointed! I'm going to be king! I don't really do the pizza-delivery thing. One day I'll have servants who do that sort of thing for me, so you'll just have to find someone else to run your errand while I practice my curtsy."

Instead of boasting in the position he'd been promised, David embraced the opportunity that was placed in front of him. And because he was patient with the process, he was presented with the opportunity to face and defeat Goliath. If he'd been impatient, he would have wound up "waiting to be discovered" while sulking at home, thus forfeiting his opportunity.

BE PATIENT WITH THE PEOPLE

If we're going to be effective leaders, we also need to learn how to be patient with difficult people—especially those who are above us on the org chart.

Let me fill you in on a secret about any organization, whether it's a home, a business, or a ministry: everyone has a difficult time with their boss, because there's no such thing as a perfect leader. When people are dealing with a difficult situation in the leadership of their organization, they often get impatient and walk out or move on to something new just so they won't have to put up with the crap anymore.

I'm not saying there's never a time to consider a new place of employment or a new place to serve. However, I am saying that when we endure difficult circumstances, persevering through the struggle can actually serve an awesome purpose, because it teaches us how we should and should not lead people once we are in a leadership position ourselves. By walking away every time we face a difficult season, we may actually be walking away from discovering our potential in the process.

After David proved himself to be patient with the process, he received a promotion. What leader doesn't love a promotion? This means being in charge of more people, being able to make more decisions, and having more influence and opportunities. (And sometimes, more money!)

However, this advancement also requires patience, since leaders often experience resistance rather than reward at this point.

Resistance can come in the form of jealousy from coworkers. Other times resistance comes as a result of self-doubt. And sometimes resistance is simply from an increase in responsibilities, which inevitably increases the pressure on our lives.

Following David's victory over Goliath, David began leading the armies of Israel whenever they went to battle. He was receiving attention from his fellow Israelites—way more than Saul was getting, which made Saul incredibly jealous.

Saul's anger reached such levels that Saul actually tried to kill David—twice!

The next day an evil spirit from God came forcefully on Saul. He was prophesying in his house, while David was playing the lyre, as he usually did. Saul had a spear in his hand and he hurled it, saying to himself, "I'll pin David to the wall." But David eluded him twice.

I SAMUEL 18:10-11

Saul's insecurity was eating him alive. (There's nothing more discouraging than working for an insecure leader.) But David didn't quit; he didn't lead a rebellion. Instead, he embraced the process and stayed with his job—even after his boss tried to murder him!

Finally, one day Saul gave David an assignment that, if it weren't in the Bible, I wouldn't believe anyone would ask another person to do.

Let me set this up.

Saul wanted David to marry his daughter, thinking that if David were his son-in-law, perhaps he would be easier to keep in check. David refused the first daughter the king offered him; however, Scripture says he actually liked Saul's second daughter. So

Saul gave David this assignment so he could receive the promotion to son-in-law:

> Saul replied, "Say to David, 'The king wants no other price for the bride than a hundred Philistine foreskins, to take revenge on his enemies.'" Saul's plan was to have David fall by the hands of the Philistines.
>
> When the attendants told David these things, he was pleased to become the king's son-in-law. So before the allotted time elapsed, David took his men with him and went out and killed two hundred Philistines and brought back their foreskins. They counted out the full number to the king so that David might become the king's son-in-law. Then Saul gave him his daughter Michal in marriage.
>
> I SAMUEL 18:25-27

You may think your boss has asked you to do some crazy things, but I'm not sure anyone has a story to top this one. A hundred foreskins from your country's most feared enemy? I would have told Saul he had lost his dang mind and then headed to the nearest job fair.

However, instead of complaining or gossiping in the break room about what a horrible boss Saul was, David went out and accomplished twice as much as Saul had asked for, getting not the one hundred as requested but going above and beyond and collecting two hundred. Talk about the extra mile!

Great leaders don't embrace only the jobs that will get them a lot of attention; rather, they're willing to do whatever it takes to advance the greater cause. Was this David's dream job? Is this what he'd imagined doing since he was a little boy? Probably not! But instead of whining about it, he showed patience with this difficult person in his life. And the lessons he learned while under Saul's leadership helped him become an effective king.

Eventually David had to leave "Saul & Sons Inc." after Saul tried on numerous other occasions to kill him. Saul serves as a sad example to all of us that impatient and insecure leaders eventually isolate themselves, become ineffective, and make decisions that hurt other people.

David finally went out and started his own company, although the employees he had working for him weren't exactly at the top of their classes.

> David left Gath and escaped to the cave of Adullam. When his brothers and his father's household heard about it, they went down to him there. All those who were in distress or in debt or discontented gathered around him, and he became their commander. About four hundred men were with him.
>
> I SAMUEL 22:1-2

You've got to be kidding! After all David had been through, after all he'd fought for, after all he'd been promised, and with all the potential in his life, *this* was the group of people he had around him? A bunch of guys who were broke and unemployed and on the run?

Most people in David's situation would have thrown up their hands and quit. Not only was a psychopath trying to kill him, but now he had to lead the biggest group of misfits in recorded history.

However, David not only embraced the process but patiently led the people he'd been given stewardship over. Eventually some of these men who surrounded him when he was in a cave would surround him when he was in the palace—all because he was willing to take the time to develop them to become great leaders. He gave them a bigger vision: not to get a nicer cave, but to prepare to lead a kingdom. Being patient with people is more bearable when we understand that they're in the process of developing as well.

But sometimes it takes longer for the team to get there than the leader would hope.

Several years ago, I thought I had an idea that would revolutionize the things we did in our church and enable us to care for people more effectively. I thought through the plan and spent a month brainstorming and developing the concept. When I had the vision pretty clearly nailed down, I knew it was time to reveal it to my leadership team. I imagined that after my incredible presentation, they would lift me onto their shoulders and carry me around the office, declaring me one of the most innovative leaders in the world.

I rolled into the meeting that day, spent about ten minutes unpacking the amazing idea, and then waited for their response.

Nothing!

Literally, no one said a word. They all looked at me as if I'd just tried to convince them that Area 51 really is a secret UFO base and we were all in danger of being overtaken by an alien race.

Desperate to get them excited, I shared the idea again, with more passion, more ambition, more volume.

This time they didn't respond with silence; they responded with questions—lots of them.

I left that meeting incredibly frustrated. Actually, frustrated isn't the most honest description. I was angry—really angry—at my team. *Maybe I have the wrong people around me,* I thought. I began to mentally dismiss each person as either not as spiritual or not as smart as I was.

Then, as I was driving home that evening, it hit me.

I'd taken a month to think through the idea.

I'd written about it, brainstormed about it, prayed about it. And in the course of that month, my heart for the idea grew until it became a white-hot passion that consumed me.

My team, however, didn't have a month to get excited about the idea the way I had.

The problem wasn't them—it was me. I wanted my team to get excited about the idea in twenty minutes when it had taken me an entire month to get there. As a leader, I had to learn to be patient with them as they worked through the process.

* * *

If you want to accomplish the big goals that are burning in your heart, be patient with the process and embrace the responsibilities in front of you right now instead of wishing you had something better or different.

And if you want people to buy into your leadership and follow you, be patient with them. Give them room to ask questions, make mistakes, and learn as they go.

Excellent leaders know that great leadership can't be microwaved. Respect the process and the people, and trust God to unfold His plans in His perfect timing.

QUESTIONS TO HELP YOU LEAD IN THE MOST EXCELLENT WAY

Take some time to think through the questions below, both as an individual and as a team. In the next week or so, commit to making this chapter's leadership principle more of a conviction in your day-to-day decisions.

Questions to Ask Yourself

1. When do I tend to get impatient with the process? How can I stay more focused on the long-range vision?
2. Under what circumstances do I tend to get impatient with the people I lead? What are some questions I can ask myself to see things from their perspectives?

Questions to Ask Your Team

1. Do you feel I am patient with you? Why or why not?
2. What are some steps we can take to create a culture of patience here?
3. In what area do you feel I have the most room to improve when it comes to patience?

SUMMARY STATEMENTS

$\rightarrow$ An impatient leader will eventually become an ineffective leader.

$\rightarrow$ People often want the position, but they won't take the posture that causes them to become a great leader.

$\rightarrow$ Patiently embrace the process, and the process will put you in a position to succeed.

$\rightarrow$ Embrace the responsibilities in front of you right now instead of wishing you had something better or different.

#BestWayToLead

CHAPTER 3

KIND

Love is kind.
I CORINTHIANS 13:4

I WAS IN SERIOUS TROUBLE.

The first church I served in as a part-time youth pastor had an annual vacation Bible school week, when kids were brought to church in the evening and dropped off to learn Bible stories, eat snacks, and play games. I was in charge of the middle school and high school portion of the event.

The first year I was in charge, attendance was really low—as in, fewer than the number of people who think Reeboks are awesome. So when the next year rolled around, I was less than excited about taking charge of the event again.

I tried to convince the church leaders that having VBS for teenagers was a really bad idea and that we'd be much better off having them serve as volunteers with the younger children. However, I was voted down and told that not only did I have to do it, but I had to make it better than the year before.

The pressure was on, especially because I desperately wanted to impress the new pastor. He'd been hired a few months earlier, and I had a hunch he didn't like me very much. I had to come up with an idea so good that it would change everything.

Then, about a week before the kickoff, I came up with an idea that would revolutionize VBS worldwide. Seriously, it was brilliant (I thought), and it carried with it the distinct possibility of propelling me light-years ahead of the leadership track I was currently on. We were going to shatter previous attendance records and create such an impact that people would be talking about it for years.

Here's the idea. At the end of the week, I would let the teenagers have the first annual VBS food fight. They would be allowed to bring anything they wanted—nothing was off limits.

I didn't tell the pastor, because I wanted him to see the results for himself and be in awe of the amazing, innovative leader on his team.

The night of the food fight we had record attendance. In fact, we had the most students we'd ever had in the church building at the same time. I just knew this was my big breakthrough and figured I'd probably receive some sort of award.

One kid brought several bottles of mustard, another brought a gallon of milk that he'd let sit in the sun all week, and several students brought raw eggs. This thing was shaping up to be epic!

We all went outside after I taught a Bible study no one paid attention to, and finally I gave the cue. Food began flying everywhere.

There were so many students and so much chaos that the food fight couldn't be contained to one location. Eventually the kids moved from the parking lot to the graveyard behind the church.

Looking back now, I can see that this wasn't actually the best idea. But in the moment, I thought it was *awesome*. I had a dozen eggs with me, and I'd slam a kid in the face with one and then duck behind a tombstone before anyone could retaliate.

By the end of the food fight, the graveyard looked like a tornado had hit a grocery store. There were Vienna sausages lying on

Mr. Smith's grave (I think he died in the 1800s), eggs dripping from Mrs. Trotter's marker, and chocolate syrup smeared all over Mr. and Mrs. Thomas's tombstone.

Honestly, I didn't figure anyone in the graveyard would mind. After all, they were dead—they didn't care.

After the melee was over, I strolled back to the church to wash myself off with a hose before changing my clothes. That's when I saw him. The pastor.

To say he was slightly unhappy would be like saying the Pope is slightly Catholic.

His face was as red as the ketchup that had just been flying through the air, and he was shaking his head in disbelief.

After just looking at me for a minute or so, he walked away without saying a word.

I'm not the sharpest knife in the drawer, but in that particular moment I realized that I was in trouble.

I waited about fifteen minutes and then called the pastor at his house. I was sure I could smooth things over. After all, he was a pastor, right? It's pretty much his job to extend grace to the people on his staff. There's no way something like this was going to get me in too much trouble.

I had never been more wrong.

As soon as he heard my voice, he began screaming at me, telling me I had "compromised the Gospel" and saying something about my being a heretic. To top it off, he said he'd never been more ashamed of anyone who worked for him. At first I thought it was a joke, but after about ten seconds, I realized I was in deep weeds with this man!

After he berated me about the food fight in the graveyard, he started in on all the other things I'd done in the short time he'd been there that had made him mad, such as the way I taught the

Bible, which version of the Bible I used, and the "devil music" I listened to. He kept yelling for another ten minutes or so, and then he said, "Now don't call me back." He slammed the phone down, and I was left with a dial tone in my ear.

I remember sitting in my office, staring at the wall. At that moment, I made a decision: I would do my best to never treat anyone who worked with me or for me the way he'd just treated me.

We learn from the examples set before us—sometimes they're models we want to follow, and sometimes they're ones we *don't* want to follow. In this case, I learned an important lesson about kindness (or, more accurately, the opposite of kindness).

The second thing Paul says about love-based leadership is that "love is kind" (1 Corinthians 13:4).

Now, I'll admit *kindness* isn't a word that's thrown around in many leadership circles. Kindness sounds weak. It brings to mind meetings filled with group hugs and incense. It seems to fit better with rainbows, unicorns, and leprechauns than with vision statements and board meetings.

But in reality, kindness is essential to great leadership.

Let me share with you four truths about kindness that I believe will help us develop into excellent leaders.

THE "WHO" IS MORE IMPORTANT THAN THE "WHAT"

Kindness means that we're more concerned with who a person is becoming than what they're doing. If the pastor at my first church had been focused on my character and had sat down with me, calmly explained why he had an issue with what I'd done, and not used the incident to unload all his pent-up frustrations, I would have benefited greatly. And I think the pastor would have too.

Caring about people isn't good just for the people you lead; it's good for you, too.

In the early days of NewSpring Church, when our staff was made up of only a handful of people, we would all go to lunch after our staff meetings on Tuesdays. As I look back on that era now, I realize that the time I spent with my team, hearing about their families and friends, laughing about hilarious life stories, and finding out what they liked and disliked, gave me more leadership leverage than when I sat behind a desk and gave them assignments and tried to "drop some wisdom" on them.

A number of years ago, I heard John Maxwell say, "People don't care how much you know until they know how much you care." When I first heard those words, I honestly thought it was a dumb idea; after all, I didn't have time to light candles, put on a toga, and run around giving people hugs and lollipops. But now I realize it's one of the most important leadership principles a person can put into practice.

As leaders, we often get so hyperfocused on results that we press on at a ridiculous speed. And while we may achieve what we set out to do, we leave behind a wake of distrust because people feel used and abused rather than valued and appreciated.

This is true for every aspect of leadership, at every level. If you're a parent, one of the best things you can do is to care more about who your children are becoming than what they're doing. At sporting events, I've seen parents who yell derogatory comments at their children because they aren't doing what the parents expect them to do. Those parents may succeed in making their children a little better in their athletic performances, but they'll fail at communicating to their kids that who they are as people is more important than their batting averages.

The same principle applies if you own a small business, lead a church, or happen to be the CEO of a Fortune 500 company: the best way to maintain excellent employees is to care more about who they are becoming than what they are doing.

This means taking the time to slow down and have conversations with people rather than looking past them to your next task or your next conversation. This means doing little things that are actually big things, like setting up some sort of system that informs you when the people on your team have birthdays, anniversaries, or other special events.

I know the argument here: "I don't have time for all that touchy-feely crap. We have to get stuff done. I pay these people to work."

That's true. As a matter of fact, if you take a look at your budget, employee payroll is likely the largest line item. As leaders, we have to understand that people are our greatest asset and therefore our greatest investment. Wouldn't you want to make sure you're getting the greatest return on that investment?

People may join a company or organization because they believe in the cause, but they will often leave, not because they don't believe in the cause anymore, but because they believe the leader doesn't care about them.

However, if the people who work for you believe you really care about them, they'll stick it out and do whatever it takes, even in the midst of intense seasons, to make sure the work gets done.

KINDNESS AND CORRECTION GO HAND IN HAND

Kindness doesn't mean we avoid having difficult conversations with people.

Kindness doesn't mean we refuse to address poor performance.

Kindness demands that we tell the truth.

Recently a friend of mine went on a new diet and decided to

make some healthy cookies. She has about as much experience with baking as I have flying a spaceship, so this was destined to go poorly from the beginning.

She made the cookies and asked her roommate to try one. The roommate took a bite, and her body tried to defend itself by convincing her to get the cookie out of her mouth as soon as possible.

However, instead of spitting the cookie across the room, she chewed and swallowed and then said, with a smile on her face, "These cookies are amazing!"

The next day the cookie maker decided to take some of her awesome new cookies to work and bless her coworkers with them. After all, according to her roommate, they were "amazing."

Needless to say, the people in her office didn't feel the same pressure to make her feel like an excellent pastry chef.

While her roommate thought she was being kind, she was actually being cruel, because she set her friend up for failure. As leaders, we have the responsibility of speaking the truth (in kindness, of course) so the people we lead don't become the emperor with no clothes.

The way Jesus dealt with people—even when they made enormous mistakes—serves as an example to every leader on the planet of how to correct others with kindness.

The Bible describes a mob of people coming to arrest Jesus and put Him on trial. It was a tense situation, and His disciples were ready for anything to happen.

> Simon Peter, who had a sword, drew it and struck the high priest's servant, cutting off his right ear. (The servant's name was Malchus.)
>
> Jesus commanded Peter, "Put your sword away! Shall I not drink the cup the Father has given me?"

JOHN 18:10-11

I don't think I'm stretching things here when I say that cutting off Malchus's ear was not a part of the plan. Peter had obviously messed up. He acted on impulse. He made a mistake, and now there was blood on the ground.

And that's when we see Jesus step in and, with kindness, correct Peter.

Some people read into this account that Jesus was lecturing Peter and tearing him down in front of the other disciples. But when we look at the life of Jesus, it's obvious that this interpretation is inconsistent with His character and the way He treated people.

I think Jesus was speaking to Peter in a low tone of voice here, almost a whisper. He loved Peter enough to correct him and respected him enough not to rip him apart in front of his friends.

After Jesus and Peter had their little heart-to-heart, Jesus put the servant's ear back on. This serves as an excellent example for us as leaders to step back in a situation, speak correction when necessary, and then do what we can to make the situation better.

Peter didn't get fired after his slipup. In fact, it was Peter who had the privilege of preaching the very first message ever given in the church following Jesus' resurrection.

Isn't it funny how the guy who made a huge mistake turned out to be one of the MVPs of the early church—all because he had a leader who loved him enough to correct him with kindness?

KINDNESS MUST BE INTENTIONAL

We have to make a conscious effort to be kind, because position and success can deceive us into thinking we no longer need to be kind to people. One of the myths in the leadership world is that the higher a person climbs, the less kind they have to be.

All of us have seen, if not experienced firsthand, examples of this.

One of the excuses leaders often use for not being kind is "I'm busy."

I get it!

I feel this tension on a daily basis. As someone who is responsible for a church with more than four hundred employees and a budget of more than $50 million, who also happens to have a wife and a little girl I love, I know what it's like to have a to-do list that never ends and a phone that never stops buzzing.

Busy is a word I often use to describe my life, and my guess is that the same is true for you.

However, if we aren't careful, we can become so busy doing leadership-type activities that we're no longer effective in our leading.

When the schedule becomes more important than the people in our lives, we're in trouble.

I came face-to-face with this reality last year.

I was scheduled to show up at a lunch, spend about an hour with a group of teenagers, and then proceed to the next event. I was on a student trip in Israel, and it was important to stay on schedule so we could make all our destinations.

I arrived at the restaurant just in time, sat down with the group of teenagers, and began chatting. But the whole time I was watching the clock.

About forty-five minutes into the conversation, as I was getting ready to wrap things up and rush out the door so I could stay on schedule, the fifteen-year-old girl sitting beside me, who had been a bit fidgety the entire lunch, said, "Pastor P., can I ask you a question?"

"Sure," I responded.

"What do you do when there are people in your life you really care about who are making bad decisions? You just want them to give their lives to Christ and become a new person, but they won't change."

Then she began crying. And not just a few tears—she was sobbing uncontrollably.

My first instinct was to get someone to pray with her so I could stick to the schedule; after all, I was busy. I was the leader—I had lessons to teach and responsibilities to deal with. However, in that moment, I felt the Holy Spirit press into me that I needed to put my schedule aside.

I sat there for the next hour and listened to her, prayed with her, and encouraged her. I have to admit, at first I didn't want to. However, the Lord used that event in my life to remind me that I should never consider myself so important that I can't slow down and minister in the moment when given the opportunity.

Jesus was the busiest leader on the planet. Talk about an agenda—He had places to go, things to do, and a world to save, yet He seemed to have time for children, lepers, and outcasts. His kindness impacted people in ways that are still being talked about today. Who knows—maybe our small acts of kindness will be the most significant legacy we leave behind.

WE NEED TO ALLOW PEOPLE TO MAKE MISTAKES

Whenever I have the urge to be unkind to someone for something they've said or done, I try to stop and remember how many times I've said or done something foolish and how people have shown me kindness rather than condemnation in those moments.

When I hired a campus pastor for one of our locations, he asked me for a bit of advice as he started in his position. I told him, "You're going to make major mistakes. You're going to cost this church a ton of money. And that's okay, because I've made major mistakes and cost this church a lot of money too."

If you are a Christian, kindness isn't just a good idea; it's a command. As the Bible puts it, "Be kind and compassionate to one another, forgiving each other, just as in Christ God forgave you" (Ephesians 4:32). Leaders who model forgiveness and allow people second chances build a culture people love to work in.

* * *

Jesus said, "A new command I give you: Love one another. As I have loved you, so you must love one another. By this everyone will know that you are my disciples, if you love one another" (John 13:34-35).

Did you catch that? Jesus said the way the world will know we belong to Him is by the way we love one another.

That doesn't mean that we don't become angry but that we show genuine kindness even when there's conflict.

That doesn't mean that we allow poor performance to go unnoticed but that when we address it, we do so with kindness, out of concern for the person.

That doesn't mean that we ignore character flaws or mistakes in a person but that we deal with them in a manner that is kind and nonjudgmental.

When I think about the memorable teachers I've had in my life, some of the names that pop into my mind are Miss Kellet (first grade), Mrs. Hancock (sixth grade), Mrs. Kay (seventh grade), and Mrs. Jones (tenth grade).

Why do I remember them specifically?

Because they were outstanding teachers?

Because of their superior knowledge?

Because they made lots of money?

No—it's because they were some of the kindest people I've met in my life.

I'm sure the same is true for you—the reason certain teachers and leaders had an impact on you is most likely because they were kind. We may grow up, but we never outgrow our need for kind leaders.

Kindness isn't for soft leaders, and it's not a sign of weakness. It's a sign of strength, and it's an essential trait for anyone who wants to lead in the most excellent way.

QUESTIONS TO HELP YOU LEAD IN THE MOST EXCELLENT WAY

Questions to Ask Yourself

1. Who are some of the kindest people I know? What do they do to show kindness to me and the other people around them?
2. Who can I show kindness to in the next week? What are some specific acts of kindness I could show them?

Questions to Ask Your Team

1. Do you think I care more about who you are becoming than what you are doing? Why or why not?
2. Is this a place where it's okay to make mistakes? What can we do to make the culture here a kinder one?

SUMMARY STATEMENTS

→ Kindness means that we're more concerned with who a person is becoming than with what they're doing.

→ As leaders, we have to understand that people are our greatest asset and therefore our greatest investment.

→ Kindness demands that we tell the truth.

→ If we aren't careful, we can become so busy doing leadership-type activities that we're no longer effective in our leading.

→ Maybe our small acts of kindness will be the most significant legacy we leave behind.

#BestWayToLead

CHAPTER 4

DOES NOT ENVY

Love . . . does not envy.
1 CORINTHIANS 13:4

I CANNOT STAND THE NEW YORK YANKEES.

For me, the best season in baseball ever would be if they went 0–162.

Every time I see someone wearing a New York Yankees hat, I confess I want to knock it off their head.

If you're a Yankees fan and are offended by these statements, I am not going to apologize.

Yes, I know that historically and statistically, the Yankees are the best team in baseball, having won twenty-seven titles, which accounts for 25 percent of all series played and 43 percent of the wins claimed by American League teams.

I know that Babe Ruth, Derek Jeter, and Reggie Jackson (as well as dozens of other Yankees players) are among some of the greatest athletes to ever play the game.

I've been told that a game in Yankee Stadium (especially against the Red Sox) is one of the greatest events a sports fan could experience.

However, in spite of all of this, I can't stand the team.

Why?

It's simple: because I'm an Atlanta Braves fan. And as much as I hate to admit it, the Yankees have always been the better team.

I'm still bitter about the World Series in 1996, when the Braves were up 2–0 in the series and then went on to lose four straight to the "Bronx Bombers."

The reason for my hatred of the Yankees is envy, pure and simple. I wish the team I cheered for won more frequently and had more World Series victories to celebrate. I wish they did more than make it to the play-offs year after year only to quit playing once they got there.

While we can laugh at my envy over the Yankees, envy is no laughing matter when it comes to leadership. It's the root cause for unhealthy comparison, unnecessary attacks, and wasted energy in a church, business, or family.

The next thing Paul says about the most excellent way to lead is that "love . . . does not envy" (1 Corinthians 13:4).

Envy is something we need to be constantly on the lookout for and ready to yank out. If we allow it to take root in our hearts and minds, it will make us—and the organizations we lead—unhealthy and unfocused.

It's easy to become so envious of what seems to be going well for other leaders that we lose sight of how much we have to be thankful for in our own situations.

Paul deals with the subject of envy and comparison in a number of his writings. In his second letter to the Corinthian church, he writes, "Oh, don't worry; we wouldn't dare say that we are as wonderful as these other men who tell you how important they are! But they are only comparing themselves with each other, using themselves as the standard of measurement. How ignorant!" (2 Corinthians 10:12, NLT).

This is a strong message—but a necessary one. The comparison trap can make us so obsessed with others that we try to imitate what they're doing instead of initiating what we're supposed to be doing. God gives unique gifts and a unique call to each leader, so it's pointless to stress over someone else's talent or popularity or budget or church size. We're simply asked to be faithful to what we've been called to do.

In his letter to the Galatians, Paul says, "The same God who worked through Peter as the apostle to the Jews also worked through me as the apostle to the Gentiles" (Galatians 2:8, NLT).

In other words, God is God. He worked through Peter in one way to lead one group of people, and He worked through Paul in a completely different way to lead another group of people. The differences were not criticized but celebrated.

Galatians 6:4 says, "Pay careful attention to your own work, for then you will get the satisfaction of a job well done, and you won't need to compare yourself to anyone else" (NLT).

Envy robs us of the satisfaction the Lord wants us to experience as a result of a job well done. We simply can't enjoy the things we've been blessed with and the people we're called to lead if we're envious of what others have that we don't.

Envy has a number of dangers, and here we'll talk about four of them. It's essential for us to recognize how destructive envy can be so we can make sure it doesn't take root in our hearts.

ENVY STIFLES CELEBRATION

Several years ago some friends I work with got together and bought me my very first big-screen TV—one with a surround-sound system. They had it installed in my house while I was on vacation, and to say I was surprised, overwhelmed, and grateful when I walked in the door would be a huge understatement. For the next several months, I had to pinch myself whenever I turned on my TV. I couldn't believe how much I'd been blessed.

Then it happened—*it* being the day I visited a friend's house and saw his new TV.

It was awesome!

It was thinner than mine.

It had a better picture.

It had better sound.

And I hated it.

When I saw it mounted on the wall so perfectly, I remember thinking, *I hope it falls off the wall and shatters into a zillion pieces.*

On the way home that night, I contemplated how pathetic my TV was and how underwhelming my surround sound was and how much I deserved the better TV. Gently but directly, however, Jesus began dealing with my heart, reminding me that not only was the TV a gift but He'd given me so many other things I didn't deserve, like the living room the TV goes in and the friends who got it for me in the first place. And then He whispered to my heart that there are billions of people in the world who have way more significant problems than having a friend who has a nicer TV than they do.

Envy caused me to be unable to celebrate what my friend had. And it made me forget how much I have to be grateful for.

When it comes to the success of the people we lead and work or serve with, we have a choice: we can criticize them because we're jealous of their accomplishments, or we can celebrate alongside them. We can't do both.

Let's go back to the story about Saul and David.

When the victorious Israelite army was returning home after David had killed the Philistine, women from all the towns of Israel came out to meet King Saul. They sang

and danced for joy with tambourines and cymbals. This
was their song:

"Saul has killed his thousands,
 and David his ten thousands!"

This made Saul very angry. "What's this?" he said.
"They credit David with ten thousands and me with only
thousands. Next they'll be making him their king!" So
from that time on Saul kept a jealous eye on David.

1 SAMUEL 18:6-9, NLT

In this story we see the Israelite army coming back from a victory. This was a huge deal—thousands of Israelites had been saved,
and the nation had been spared from destruction.

A massive celebration began. The Bible says that the women
started dancing and singing. Apparently Saul loved it . . . until he
listened to the lyrics of the song: "Saul has killed his thousands,
and David his ten thousands!"

It seems that this song was what pushed Saul over the edge.

The very next day a tormenting spirit from God
overwhelmed Saul, and he began to rave in his house
like a madman. David was playing the harp, as he
did each day. But Saul had a spear in his hand, and
he suddenly hurled it at David, intending to pin him
to the wall. But David escaped him twice.

1 SAMUEL 18:10-11, NLT

Envy drove Saul to want to kill David.

Just think about how differently this situation could have turned out. What if Saul had heard the song and, instead of lamenting that David killed nine times more men than he did, he said, "Wow, look how many men David and I killed together!"

What if Saul could have celebrated David's success instead of making it all about himself? What if he'd joined in the song instead of trying to kill his competition?

I think the story could have turned out much better for everyone—especially Saul.

One of the most dangerous pitfalls in leadership is when leaders become envious of someone who reports to them. When they react out of jealousy, they tend to tear down rather than build up, assume the worst rather than the best, and push others away rather than draw them in.

This isn't just true for pastors and CEOs; it applies to parents as well. Have you ever seen parents who can't celebrate the success of someone else's child because doing so would be admitting that their child was outperformed?

It's only when leaders learn to celebrate the success of others that they can lead in the most excellent way.

ENVY LEADS TO INSANITY

I used to run about five miles a day—and I actually enjoyed it.

Several years ago, along with a group of my friends, I decided to train for a marathon. For the first several weeks, I was feeling pretty good about myself, because I was always the first person in the group to cross the finish line.

Then a friend of one of the people in the group found out we were running together, and she asked if she could join us for one of our longer runs one Saturday. That was fine with us, so the next

Saturday she showed up and stretched with the group before we headed to the starting point together.

When we began the run, I noticed that the new runner was slightly faster than I was. (After the run, I was told she had been on the cross-country team in college.) As the run progressed, I fell farther and farther behind.

Finally I decided that things were not going to go down like this. I was the fastest runner in our group, and I wasn't going to let the new girl show me up.

I picked up the pace and started pushing myself beyond my limit. And for a while at least, it worked. I was closing the gap on the distance between us, and I began having dreams of smiling and waving as I passed her.

However, those dreams were short lived.

The last part of our run was up a hill, and because I had pursued insanity, my body rebelled and I caught a cramp. Now, this wasn't a small cramp; it was a "Dear God, please take my life right now" cramp.

I had pursued insanity and paid the price.

(I also never told her when our group was running again!)

When we begin to focus on—or even obsess over—those who are doing things better, faster, more effectively, or more glamorously than we are, we lose focus on what we've been called to do. We also begin to set unrealistic goals for ourselves and our teams.

Saul wasted so much time being jealous of David that he lost sight of leading his kingdom, until eventually he lost everything.

Leadership is stewardship. One day when we stand before God, we'll be held accountable for whether we were obedient to the calling and resources He placed in our lives. We are not responsible for how other people run their races; we are only responsible for how we run our own.

In John 11–12 we find another example of how envy leads to insanity. A guy named Lazarus, one of Jesus' friends, became sick, and within a few days he died. Jesus made His way to the funeral, and long story short, He raised Lazarus from the dead. A massive celebration took place (and rightfully so).

But not everyone was happy about this miracle. The group of religious leaders called the Pharisees were incredibly envious of Jesus. Many people had started following Him, and they didn't like that He was taking the spotlight off them.

> Some went to the Pharisees and told them what Jesus had done. Then the leading priests and Pharisees called the high council together. "What are we going to do?" they asked each other. "This man certainly performs many miraculous signs. If we allow him to go on like this, soon everyone will believe in him. Then the Roman army will come and destroy both our Temple and our nation."
> JOHN 11:46-48 (NLT)

Instead of celebrating the miracle, the Pharisees held a meeting. Instead of celebrating what Jesus had done, they were worried about their own popularity. And this caused them to pursue insanity.

> When all the people heard of Jesus' arrival, they flocked to see him and also to see Lazarus, the man Jesus had raised from the dead. Then the leading priests decided to kill Lazarus, too, for it was because of him that many of the people had deserted them and believed in Jesus.
> JOHN 12:9-11 (NLT)

Think about it—this was a classic case of insanity!

Why?

Lazarus had already been dead once. How did the priests think they could intimidate him with the threat of death? I'm thinking he would have said, "Go ahead—give it a shot. Been there, done that."

The religious leaders became so obsessed with knowing someone was greater than they were that they poured themselves into destroying the very people they were supposed to serve.

In business or in ministry, when we focus on what others are doing and measure our success against theirs, it causes us to lose sight of our calling and mission. It also leads to frustration, disappointment, and burnout. And insanity is the result every single time.

ENVY PROMOTES THE LIE THAT LIFE IS FAIR

Let me fill you in on a phrase I commonly say to my staff: "Fair is a place where you ride rides."

We all have an innate desire for justice, which is a good thing, but real justice doesn't mean that everyone gets treated exactly the same.

If you spend all your effort trying to make sure everything is completely fair (whether as a leader or a follower), you are setting yourself up for disappointment.

If the leader in your group or organization seems to spend more time with one person or one particular group of people than they do with you, it's easy to jump to the conclusion "That's not fair!" And if you're a leader whose priority is to try to keep everyone happy instead of doing the right thing, you'll bend over backward trying to accommodate the people who are making accusations against you.

This is a recipe for disaster.

Jesus was good, but that doesn't mean He was fair.

Think about it: Scripture says He had a group of seventy-two followers (see Luke 10:1). Out of the seventy-two, He had a group of twelve, called apostles (see Matthew 10:1). Out of the twelve apostles, there were three (Peter, James, and John) He seemed to favor more than the others, as they were often the only ones to witness certain miracles (see Matthew 17:1-13; 26:36-38). And then out of those three, there was "the one Jesus loved" (John 20:2), so it seems even Jesus had favorites.

Jesus was an unparalleled leader, and one of the reasons for that was because He refused to allow others' envy to direct His decisions.

Jesus exposes the fairness lie in one of His parables:

The Kingdom of Heaven can be illustrated by the story of a man going on a long trip. He called together his servants and entrusted his money to them while he was gone. He gave five bags of silver to one, two bags of silver to another, and one bag of silver to the last—dividing it in proportion to their abilities. He then left on his trip.
MATTHEW 25:14-15 (NLT)

Isn't it interesting that Jesus says one person received five bags of silver, another got two bags, and yet another was given one bag? Each person was blessed, but each person wasn't blessed in an equal manner.

As leaders, we must spend more time with certain people or groups than we do with others. That doesn't mean that we're evil or even that we're showing favoritism. It just means we take our callings seriously and refuse to allow those who buy into the lie of fairness to dominate our agendas.

ENVY KEEPS US IN THE CRAB BASKET

A friend of mine once told a story about crabs that I'll never forget. He said that as a kid, he met a guy who lived near the Atlantic Ocean, where people sometimes go out and catch crabs for dinner. The guy informed my friend that when he went out to catch crabs, he needed a bucket with a lid on it so that when he caught a crab, the lid would prevent it from crawling out. The man went on to explain, though, that if you catch two or more crabs, you don't need a lid anymore. My friend was confused until the man explained that if you have two or more crabs in the basket, every time one crab gets near the top, the other crabs pull him back down.

Envy causes us to do the same thing. If we get hung up on comparing our success (or lack of success) to the success of others, we tend to pull people down to our level instead of being encouraged by what they're doing and allowing it to produce a healthy drive in us.

* * *

Envy can lead people to play political games, embrace mediocrity, make excuses, and become known for what they're against rather than what they stand for.

Not only does envy hold leaders back, it paralyzes the entire organization. If we can learn to celebrate the successes of others, keep our eyes on the unique calling we've been given, and replace envy with gratitude, we'll be one step closer to leading in the most excellent way.

QUESTIONS TO HELP YOU LEAD IN THE MOST EXCELLENT WAY

Questions to Ask Yourself

1. When was the last time I paused and truly thanked God for everything He has given me?
2. Is there someone I'm jealous of whom I need to build up rather than tear down?
3. When was the last time I legitimately celebrated the success of someone else?
4. Am I trying to be fair rather than focusing on being faithful?

Questions to Ask Your Team

1. Does our organization have a culture of celebration?
2. What can we do this week to cultivate celebration in our organization?

SUMMARY STATEMENTS

→ The comparison trap can make us imitate what other people are doing instead of initiating what we're supposed to be doing.

→ It's only when leaders learn to celebrate the success of others that they can lead in the most excellent way.

→ If you spend all your effort trying to make sure everything is completely fair, you are setting yourself up for disappointment.

→ Jesus was good, but that doesn't mean He was fair.

→ Not only does envy hold leaders back, it paralyzes the entire organization.

#BestWayToLead

CHAPTER 5

DOES NOT BOAST

Love . . . does not boast.

I CORINTHIANS 13:4

It was the Fourth of July, and my dad was taking me to a fireworks stand to buy some fireworks.

I've lived in South Carolina most of my life, and what you need to understand about people in the southeastern part of the United States is that we love to blow things up. So on holidays such as New Year's Eve and the Fourth of July, we spend hundreds of dollars at fireworks stands so we can create epic explosions in the night sky.

This particular year, my dad had consumed a beer or twelve before we left for the fireworks stand. When we arrived, there were so many options that eventually my dad pointed at a huge package with an assortment of fireworks and said to the guy behind the counter, "I'll take that."

The guy said, "Yes, sir," and then followed up with this question: "Do y'all need to know how to use any of this stuff?"

Dad proceeded to lecture the guy about his vast knowledge of fireworks—how they're made and how they work. He finished with a statement to this effect: "I sure don't need a teenage boy working for minimum wage to tell me how to shoot fireworks!"

We took the package home, tore into it, and began sorting out the fireworks so we could start with the smallest explosion and gradually work our way up to the grand finale.

That's when we saw the Roman candle.

I didn't know what it was. It was clear my dad didn't either—I saw him scratching his head while we were looking at it, trying to figure out how it worked.

"Do you know what it is?" I asked.

"Uh, of course I do," he said. "Come outside, and I'll show you." So my mother, my grandmother, several aunts, uncles, and cousins, and I all went outside. We stood next to the garden my parents had planted two months before and got ready to see what a Roman candle did.

My dad held the red cylinder in one hand and used his cigar to light it.

The fuse made a hissing sound and burned closer and closer to the base.

As we all held our breath, the Roman candle began making some weird noises. My dad, not knowing what was supposed to happen, freaked out. Instinctively, he threw the firework as high in the air as he could.

I can still picture the chaos that ensued.

Flaming balls of fire began shooting all over the place, sending everyone in my family scrambling to various parts of the yard. The air was filled with the screams of adults and children alike.

The scene was straight out of a comedy movie—but this was real life! When I finally had the courage to open my eyes, I surveyed the damage. Three of the shots out of the Roman candle had landed in the garden, and the entire garden was on fire. Eventually, aside from a few scrapes and cuts and the loss of about one-fourth of the garden, things went back to normal.

My fireworks story is funny, and every time I remember it, I laugh. But the incident could have been avoided altogether if my father had simply taken the time to listen to the teenager at the fireworks stand rather than boasting about his vast knowledge of fireworks.

The next excellent bit of leadership direction Paul gives is that "love . . . does not boast" (1 Corinthians 13:4).

Boasting is one of the most common traps leaders can fall into. Leaders tend to be confident, and it's easy for that confidence to drift into overconfidence. Let's face it: as leaders, we like to brag on ourselves. We want people to know how good we are and why they should follow us.

For instance, if we're in a group talking about something good someone else has done, we'll often interject with stories of our own about how we did the same thing but had even better results. Even if we don't say anything out loud, we may be congratulating ourselves internally about how much better we are than the other person.

We've all been around leaders whose favorite subject to talk about is themselves. And leaders who are obsessed with talking about the good things they've done hardly ever brag about what their team is doing.

Since boasting comes naturally for most leaders, we need to put guardrails in place that help protect us from this temptation. There are three things we need to remember if we want to make sure boasting doesn't derail our leadership.

LEADERS NEED TO REMEMBER WHERE THEY CAME FROM

Several years ago, I was on a panel of leaders talking about the church as a whole, the challenges it faces, and the recent wins and the losses it has experienced.

The audience was allowed to ask questions at the end, and one person said, "Perry, your church has thousands of people, you're asked to preach all over the world, you write books, and you're experiencing more success than I'm sure you ever imagined. With that in mind, how do you stay humble?"

I paused for a second, and before I could answer, a massive lump formed in my throat and tears filled my eyes. It took me about thirty seconds to compose myself before I could say anything.

Finally I said, "I've never forgotten where I came from."

I know what it's like to be broke and homeless.

I know what it's like to have your furniture repossessed.

I know what it's like to not know where your next meal is coming from.

I know what it's like to be placed in remedial classes in school and told that you're not smart.

So when I look around at all that the Lord has blessed me with and all He has allowed me to do, I understand that no matter how much success people may think I've achieved, I'm just someone God, for whatever reason, has chosen to bless beyond what I deserve or comprehend.

I've never forgotten where I came from, and that keeps me pretty grounded.

A few years ago a guy I'd never heard of did something generous for our church. Our CFO gave me his name, let me know what he'd done, and asked if I knew him. I told our CFO I didn't but I'd give him a call to say thank you.

Around ten in the morning I decided to give this guy a quick call before a meeting I was about to step into.

"Hello." The voice on the other end of the phone was pretty groggy, and it was obvious that I'd just woken this dude up.

My first thought was, *What is this guy still doing in bed at 10:00 a.m.? Is he some sort of drug dealer who decided to get right with God by making a generous donation?*

"Hey, this is Pastor P.," I said. "Am I talking with Andy?"

"Yes, sir."

"Well, Andy, I'm so sorry—I can tell I just woke you up."

"No, no, it's fine," he replied. "I had my alarm set for seven so I could go in to work."

"I hate to break it to you," I said, "but if you wanted to get up at seven, you're already about three hours late."

He laughed. "Oh no, man. It's seven where I live—I'm on the West Coast."

"Are you out there on vacation?"

"No, my job has me out here for part of the year."

"Your job," I repeated. "What do you do?"

There was a long pause, and then he said, "I'm the punter for the San Francisco 49ers."

I was sitting at a computer and immediately googled the 49ers roster. I scrolled through to find the punter, and sure enough, it was him! My inner child totally geeked out. I couldn't believe I was talking to an NFL football player on the telephone!

"Hey, man, why didn't you just tell me that from the beginning?"

"I try not to make a big deal out of it," he said.

After that conversation, I had the privilege of meeting Andy and found out that he was from a small town in upstate South Carolina. He played football in high school and college and eventually pushed through to the NFL. I asked him over lunch once how he managed to stay humble after not just being a punter in the NFL but also being a Pro Bowl punter.

His reply was simple: "I've never forgotten where I came from."

If we forget where we came from, we will often lose sight of where we're going.

One of the best exercises we can do as leaders is to stop for a minute and think about how we got started. What amazing things have happened to get us to where we are? What people have taken an interest in us and given us breaks? How has God opened up doors for us to be here?

Yes, leaders may say, "I got here because I worked hard." I would raise my hand and say, "Me too." But I would also contend that the ability and desire to work hard were given to me by God. The opportunities I've been given were given to me by God. I've overcome obstacles not because I'm strong but because He is.

And while we're on the topic, I should mention that I don't believe in luck.

Luck is something people with no vision for the future sit around and wish for.

I believe there's a God who wants immeasurably more for us than we could ever ask for or imagine and who is constantly orchestrating circumstances behind the scenes. We need to acknowledge that it's His greatness, not our own, that has gotten us to where we are. If we do, then we'll be boasting in His goodness, not our own—and that's the one thing we actually have to boast about (see 1 Corinthians 1:31).

LEADERS NEED TO REMEMBER WHO THEY FOLLOW

For most people in our culture, boasting isn't considered to be a bad thing; in fact, if you want to get ahead in the corporate world, you pretty much have to boast. After all, how will the people you work with know how awesome you are unless you make them aware by bragging on yourself (or at least letting it slip on social media)?

Boasting may open a few doors for you temporarily, but in

the long term, these won't be the doors you want to go through. When we boast, we often say things about our accomplishments (or what we plan to accomplish) that are exaggerated or untrue, and that ultimately leads us down paths of pain, not success. Even if the things we're bragging about are true, people will only tolerate a narcissist for so long before they move on to the next big thing.

When we boast, we're not trying to make others' lives better. We're boasting out of selfishness and arrogance. And those are two ingredients that destroy relationships—period.

Think about marriage for a second. Would you want to be married to someone who always boasted about the things they did while criticizing all the things you failed to do? Or consider parenting. If you tell children "I told you so" over and over again, especially as they get older, you end up driving a wedge in the relationship.

The same is true in work or ministry environments. Who wants to work with the person who is always boasting about how talented they are?

It's not wrong to have gifts, but gifted people don't have to inform the world how gifted they are. They simply use their gifts, and the world can't help but notice.

Does LeBron James have to tell the world he can play basketball? No—just give him a ball, and get out of the way.

Does Beyoncé have to tell the world she can sing? Nope—just hand her a microphone and allow her to snap your head back with what her voice can do.

Boasting isn't the mark of a confident leader; it comes from a place of insecurity, doubt, and fear.

One of the most captivating stories about Jesus and His leadership is found in John 13, on the same night He would be betrayed, arrested, and ultimately handed over to be crucified. As Jesus and His apostles entered the room where they were about to share a meal together (which has become known as the Last Supper), there was no servant there to wash their feet.

This was a big deal in Jesus' day!

Washing the guests' feet was necessary, because they'd been walking around all day, often without shoes, on dusty roads covered with animal dung. Their feet were nasty. (For the record, I think feet are still nasty!)

Because this was such a dirty job, it was most often reserved for the lowest-ranking servant or slave in the household. No one of any reputation would consider washing someone's feet.

That makes this account even more powerful:

Before the Passover celebration, Jesus knew that his hour had come to leave this world and return to his Father. He had loved his disciples during his ministry on earth, and now he loved them to the very end. It was time for supper, and the devil had already prompted Judas, son of Simon Iscariot, to betray Jesus. Jesus knew that the Father had given him authority over everything and that he had come from God and would return to God. So he got up from the table, took off his robe, wrapped a towel around his waist, and poured water into a basin. Then he began to wash the disciples' feet, drying them with the towel he had around him.

JOHN 13:1-5, NLT

Jesus loved the people He led. He could have boasted in Himself (He was, after all, the Son of God), bragged about His miracles, or raved about His own teaching, but He chose not to boast but rather to serve.

Jesus' goal as a leader wasn't to impress His followers but to make sure they were served and taken care of. So He did what no one else was willing to do: He washed their feet.

Paul wrote a letter to a church in a town along the Mediterranean called Philippi. His letter includes these words:

You must have the same attitude that Christ Jesus had.

Though he was God,
    he did not think of equality with God
    as something to cling to.
Instead, he gave up his divine privileges;
    he took the humble position of a slave
    and was born as a human being.
When he appeared in human form,
    he humbled himself in obedience to God
    and died a criminal's death on a cross.

Therefore, God elevated him to the place of highest honor
    and gave him the name above all other names,
that at the name of Jesus every knee should bow,
    in heaven and on earth and under the earth,
and every tongue declare that Jesus Christ is Lord,
    to the glory of God the Father.

PHILIPPIANS 2:5-11, NLT

Scripture clearly says that Jesus gave up His rights so that those who follow Him could step into greater things.

Jesus humbled Himself, and God lifted Him up.

And God will do the same for leaders who take the posture of humility rather than the posture of pride.[2]

LEADERS NEED TO REMEMBER THAT THERE'S MORE TO DO

A friend of mine owns a restaurant in town called Sullivan's. All their food is absolutely amazing, but the thing they're really known for is their desserts. I've eaten there for years, and I have about three or four favorites, including birthday cake cheesecake, mocha Heath bar layer cake, and Kentucky Derby pie.

One night when my wife and I were eating there, I walked by the massive dessert case on my way to our table. But none of my favorites were there!

None of them!

I was disappointed, but I decided maybe I'd have to try something new.

About twenty minutes later, the owner came out of the kitchen and walked up to my table. "Earlier in the week I saw that you'd made a reservation for tonight," he said. "I know what your favorite desserts are, and I wanted to assure you that I have all three of them in the cooler in the back. So when it comes time for dessert, just let me know, and I'll make sure you get what you want."

He immediately became one of my favorite people in the world.

As I've thought about that incident, I think there are some things we can learn from it that apply to leadership.

---

[2] If you aren't a Christian, you may be arguing with me on this point; after all, you've seen some people who claim to be Christians who have been boastful and maybe even have taken advantage of you. First of all, let me acknowledge that even though a person may be a Christian, that doesn't mean they're perfect. However, let me ask you this question: If you had the opportunity to work for a leader who served like Jesus served in John 13 and who had the attitude described in Philippians 2, would you want to work for that person? I'm confident the answer is yes, which is why I contend that trying to be more like Jesus in our leadership always results in not boasting in ourselves but in being a servant of others.

When I walked into the restaurant and saw that what I wanted wasn't on display, I was disappointed. But what I didn't know was that something better was waiting for me—I just couldn't see it.

In a way, that's what it's like with God. He knows our hearts and our desires, and if He has called us to lead, then the best things He wants to do are ahead of us, not behind us.

If we believe this, then we won't waste time boasting about what we've done; instead, we'll recognize that there are greater things to come, and we'll focus our time and energy on moving toward those things.

Boastful people are often bitter because they can't stand to see someone else experience more success than they've achieved.

Humble people, however, are hungry people. They know there's more to be done. They don't mind washing feet. They don't have to be the center of attention. They embrace the fact that the best ideas are yet to be had, the best products are yet to be developed, and the best ways of doing church haven't even been discovered yet.

Humble people don't have time to brag because they're too busy serving others and striving for what's next.

One of the best ways to lead excellently is to slow down, listen to people (even the teenager at the fireworks stand), embrace humility, and wash some feet.

It worked for Jesus, and I believe it will work for us, too.

QUESTIONS TO HELP YOU LEAD IN THE MOST EXCELLENT WAY

Questions to Ask Yourself

1. What do I find myself boasting about the most?
2. Who is someone I admire as a servant-hearted leader? What makes that person stand apart from other leaders?

Questions to Ask Your Team

1. When I'm in a conversation, do I seek to make myself the center of attention?
2. What's one way I can serve you this week?

SUMMARY STATEMENTS

→ If we forget where we came from, we will often lose sight of where we're going.

→ Luck is something people with no vision for the future sit around and wish for.

→ Gifted people don't have to inform the world how gifted they are. They simply use their gifts, and the world can't help but notice.

→ If God has called you to lead, then the best things He wants to do are ahead of you, not behind you.

→ Humble people are hungry people. They know there's more to be done.

#BestWayToLead

CHAPTER 6

NOT PROUD

Love . . . is not proud.
I CORINTHIANS 13:4

I LOVE TO SEE how many plastic grocery bags I can carry at once.

I know plastic grocery bags are not PC, and I can imagine the silent lectures I'm receiving right now about the benefits of reusable bags. I'm not trying to start an argument or anything—it's just that I really like being able to have a contest with myself every time I carry groceries in plastic bags from the trunk of my car to the kitchen. I'm a little obsessed with seeing how many bags I can carry, and plastic bags just work best for that particular challenge.

I would say that 95 percent of the time (no matter how many bags there are), I can make it in one trip—even if, by the end of the journey, my body begins to go into convulsions and I begin to sweat so much that I need to change my clothes afterward.

But there's one trip I attempted several years ago that sticks out in my mind.

My wife and I lived in a dorm apartment that was provided to us by the college I was working for part-time. Lucretia had sent me to the store with a list of groceries to buy so she could prepare a special dinner for some friends we were having over.

When I was loading the bags into the car at the store, I told myself, *You can carry all these in one trip, man!*

But when I found a parking place outside our apartment and opened the trunk to get the groceries out, I began to have doubts. After all, there were a lot of groceries—including milk and eggs.

Some guys I knew walked by and saw that I had 412 pounds of groceries in my backseat. "Hey, Perry, you need a hand with those?" they asked.

The answer was yes, I did need a hand—there was no way I was going to be able to get everything inside in one trip, or even two trips. It might have even taken (gulp) three trips.

So, like a typical man in this kind of situation, I answered, "No thanks, guys. I've got it."

They shrugged and walked away, and I began to put the grocery bags all the way up each arm.

When I was halfway to our apartment, I knew I was in trouble. My heart rate was maxed out, I was sweating like a politician watching himself on YouTube, and I was on the verge of pulling a hammy.

Common sense told me to put down some of the bags and come back for them later.

But pride told me to keep going, despite the pain.

After climbing what seemed like endless flights of stairs, I realized I was going to have to either put down half of the groceries to unlock the door or try to unlock it while still holding the bags that were about to burst at the seams.

Common sense said to put them down.

Pride told me I could open the door without any negative consequences.

Right as I went to open the door, I heard the sound of ripping plastic. I just stood there, frozen. It was as if a tornado had ripped through the dairy aisle and deposited everything at our doorstep. Eggs were splattered all over the ground, and there was milk running down my right leg. And let's not even talk about what happened to the bread!

Pride had won over common sense—and as it turned out, making one trip ended up taking way more time than if I'd made multiple trips. It cost me more money, too, since I had to go back to the store and repurchase the items that had been destroyed.

This story paints a picture of what *not* to do to be an excellent leader. Allowing pride to call the shots will result in "dropped groceries" every time.

Paul's next instruction about loving leadership is that "love . . . is not proud" (1 Corinthians 13:4).

Pride is the natural tendency of any leader (or leadership team) that has experienced some sort of success in the past. When leaders are asked about the reason for their success, they like to talk about their hard work, their dedication to excellence, and their willingness to make tough decisions. However, while all those things may be true, leaders can start to take too much credit for their own success. When that happens, they are tempted to flirt with a mistress called pride. And pride will lead to a bed of death and destruction.

At a leadership talk, I once heard someone say, "One of the greatest enemies of success in our future is the success we are experiencing right now."

Pride can take root in any leader or leadership team, and if unchecked, it always leads to a downfall. As a case in point, let's take a look at Blockbuster Video.

I remember when nearly everyone I knew had a Blockbuster

card in their wallets. (If you still have a Blockbuster card in your wallet, I'm guessing you haven't cleaned out your wallet in a good five years.)

When a movie was released at Blockbuster, small riots would take place at stores all across the nation by people who were trying to obtain a copy of the movie.

If you drove by a Blockbuster store in Anytown, USA, on a Friday or Saturday night and saw the enormous crowd in the store, you would have sworn that the Blockbuster empire would never crumble.

However, pride blinded the company to the fact that it wasn't actually in the movie-rental business; it was in the entertainment business.

When Blockbuster began to hear about small start-ups like Netflix and Redbox, they dismissed them; after all, the company was making billions of dollars a year. No one on the planet was ever going to be able to touch its success.

However, on September 23, 2010, the company filed for Chapter 11 bankruptcy due to overwhelming losses. They were $900 million in debt and unable to keep up with the competition.

What killed Blockbuster wasn't that people suddenly stopped being interested in watching movies; it was pride.

Success in the past does not always equal success in the future. Many companies and organizations that were once at the top of their games are now absent from the playing field altogether.

In the 1990s a friend of mine borrowed some money from a friend and opened a storefront business in a strip mall that sold pagers (anyone remember those?). He was really success-ful in his pager sales; however, he soon realized that he wasn't actually in the pager business but rather in the communications business.

His original plan was to sell pagers and lead that particular industry for the foreseeable future, but when he realized that pagers were going the way of New Kids on the Block's music sales, he switched the entire emphasis of his company from pagers to the broader umbrella of communications.

If he had clung to the idea of pagers and simply gotten angry with everyone who was abandoning them for simpler and more economical means of communication, he would have wound up broke.

However, because he didn't allow pride to dominate his mindset, he was able to admit that his original idea wasn't perfect, and he went on to set up an extremely successful communications company. Just recently he sold it in a multimillion-dollar deal.

Believe it or not, the church is one of the most common places where pride takes root.

Imagine you were able to step into a time machine and travel back to 1980. If you looked at the top-ten largest and most effective churches in the United States at that time and compared them to today's list, you would quickly discover that none of the churches that were making a difference in 1980 are making a significant impact today.

Why is that?

Some would argue that church attendance in the United States is decreasing, and as a result, churches that were once large and influential are now small. But that argument doesn't work, because there are actually hundreds of churches all over this nation that are growing and thriving.

Others would argue that the idea of the existence of God isn't as popular as it used to be; however, basic polling data proves the opposite, as the vast majority of Americans still believe in God.

The reason so many churches have fallen from greatness is simply because they fell in love with their methods for reaching people. When people and culture began to change, these churches refused to change with them, causing them to lose relevance in people's everyday lives.

As leaders, we need to beware of and avoid three myths to ensure that pride doesn't creep into our lives and leadership.

MYTH #1: I'M THE LEADER BECAUSE I'M THE MOST INTELLIGENT

When we first began NewSpring Church, I made it a point to surround myself with people I cared about and whose opinions I valued—people who had expertise in areas that weren't my sweet spot. I understood from the beginning that if the church was going to be successful, we needed more than what was found in the six inches between my own two ears.

I'd be a liar if I didn't admit there were seasons when I thought all the people around me just didn't get it. On more than one occasion, I had the thought that all leaders have at some point: *If you want something done right, then you need to do it yourself.*

However, over time, I began to discover that whenever I thought those things, it wasn't an indictment of the people I was leading; it was actually an indictment of me.

One of the greatest assets a leader has is the people they've been blessed to lead.

When presented with a tough issue by a member of the team, the best question we can ask is "What do you think we should do?"

I've discovered that this question does four things:

1. It communicates to the people we lead that we value their opinions.
2. It often presents groundbreaking ideas that we never would have thought of on our own.

3. It exposes us to new ways of thinking about things.

4. It allows us to see who's depending on us to have the answers, and who actually knows the answer and is simply seeking permission to move forward.

Before I move on, let me quickly address the issue of age and intelligence.

Some people think the way they've always done things is the best, so they dismiss the next generation as people who simply don't get it. Other people think the newest way is always best, so they ignore the insights of people who have more life experience to draw from. Whether we're new leaders or seasoned leaders or somewhere in the middle, we should all be willing to learn from people in different age brackets.

Don't let your pride keep you from learning from people who are smarter than you!

MYTH #2: I'M THE LEADER BECAUSE I'M THE STRONGEST

Not long ago, I heard John Maxwell speak, and he shared a job description for "the perfect pastor":

After hundreds of years searching, the perfect pastor has been found. He is the church leader who will please everyone.

1. He preaches exactly twenty minutes and then sits down.

2. He condemns sin, but he never steps on anybody's toes.

3. He works from eight in the morning until ten at night, doing everything from preaching sermons to sweeping.

4. He makes $400 per week, gives $100 a week to the church, drives a late-model car, buys lots of books, wears fine clothes, and has a nice family.

5. He is always ready to contribute to every good cause, as well as help panhandlers who drop by the church.
6. He is thirty-six years old and has been preaching for forty years.
7. He is tall on the short side, heavyset in a thin sort of way, and handsome.
8. He has blue or brown eyes (to fit the occasion) and wears his wavy, straight hair parted on the middle-left right side.
9. He has a burning desire to work with the youth and spends all his time with the senior citizens.
10. He smiles all the time while keeping a straight face, because he has a keen sense of humor while being seriously dedicated.
11. He makes fifteen visits a day to church members, spends all his time evangelizing nonmembers, and is always in his study if he is needed.

Unfortunately he burned himself out and died at the age of thirty-two.

Whether or not you're in ministry, you can probably relate to the feeling that you will never be able to please everyone all the time. The "ideal leader" simply doesn't exist.

There are a lot of expectations and pressures on leaders—some of them spoken and most of them implied. We may think that being a good leader means doing everything demanded of us and keeping everyone we lead happy. However, real strength is found not in people pleasing but in posturing ourselves with humility and a willingness to ask for help.

One of the realities of being a leader is dealing with the fact that you will let people down. Unless you have the courage to disappoint people, you will never adequately lead them.

Some leaders can plow through this section because they simply don't care about people. They care about bottom lines, bonuses, attention, and prestige, and in so doing, they leave behind a wake of damaged people who once had incredible potential but were used rather than valued and appreciated.

The most excellent way to lead people isn't through control and manipulation; it's through seriously caring about them. When we care about the people we lead, it's much more difficult when we disappoint them.

Early on in our church, I had to make one of the toughest decisions I've ever made in leadership. There was someone who was amazing to be around, had extraordinary talent, and added value to a lot of what we were doing; however, he simply was not the right person to lead the area I'd placed him over. I knew the right thing to do was to release him from our staff.

I knew it was the right decision. Over time, the fact that it was the right decision was continually confirmed; however, in order to make the decision, I had to decide to disappoint some of the people who were close to me. Making the right decision also caused me to nearly throw up.

I was so tempted to hold everything in and pretend like I had it all together, but eventually I found the strength and courage to do what was right, even though it was hard.

If we try to present an image of having it all together, that pressure will eventually weigh us down. It will dominate our thinking, cause us to be dishonest in meetings, and allow the fear of man to control the way we lead.

If we are unable to be vulnerable with those we lead, we end up taking a "white-knuckle approach" to leadership: pushing through the emotional pain and refusing to admit that we're going through a tough time. We're afraid that transparency and vulnerability will make us look weak, so we hide behind a mask of false strength.

More than two decades ago, I asked a leader I respected to tell me what leaders do, and his response was immediate: "A leader always goes first."

I didn't fully appreciate what he meant at first, but over time I've come to realize that this is less glamorous than it sounds.

- Leaders are the first to admit they've made a mistake.
- Leaders are the first to admit they don't have all the answers.
- Leaders are the first to admit they're fearful or uncertain about the future.
- Leaders are the first to admit they feel as if they have the weight of the world on their shoulders.
- Leaders are the first to admit they have weaknesses—and to ask for help.

If you want to lead in a culture where people are transparent, honest, and raw, then you have to be willing to set the tone. Pretending you're strong all the time when you aren't is the fastest way to make those you're leading feel inadequate. In contrast, people who lead with vulnerability gain the trust of those who follow them.

And contrary to popular opinion, doing these things as a leader doesn't make you look weak; rather, it allows people to see you as someone they can relate to instead of "the man behind the curtain."

When it comes to vulnerability, we must make a decision: are we called to lead or to win a popularity contest?

It's okay not to feel strong; however, it's not okay to pretend you have it all together. If leaders are unhealthy, then everything they lead will be unhealthy as well. Strength doesn't mean you never have to ask for help or admit you made a mistake; strength is realizing that our weaknesses are actually someone else's strength. This allows us to lead through the strength of the team rather than through our own individual strength.

MYTH #3: I'M THE LEADER BECAUSE I'M THE HOLIEST

I have to be honest—on most days, I fall incredibly short of the Man Who Acted Most Like Jesus award.

I become way too easily frustrated with my wife and daughter.

People who cut me off in traffic make me want to say "not nice" words.

I sometimes laugh at things I shouldn't laugh at.

I often say things I shouldn't say.

I could go on and on, but I'm sure you get the point: if Jesus and I were standing side by side, I don't believe anyone would mistake us for twins.

In church culture, we sometimes get the idea that being pious paved the way for us to be in a leadership position. We assume that other people aren't leading in the same style we do because they aren't as godly as we are.

This mentality causes us to look down on those with different leadership styles than we have, and it also causes us to view those who sin with condemnation rather than compassion. This inflated self-image feeds our pride, and before long we've actually bought

into the idea that the people who follow us would be amazing people if they would learn to think and act just like us.

No one wants to follow a leader like that.

Let's return to our story about Saul, the jealous king, and David, the future leader of Israel.

Saul was planning to kill David.

Not fire him.

Not write him up.

Not launch him into another "career opportunity."

He was planning to *kill* him.

David hid in the field, and when the New Moon feast came, the king sat down to eat. He sat in his customary place by the wall, opposite Jonathan, and Abner sat next to Saul, but David's place was empty. Saul said nothing that day, for he thought, "Something must have happened to David to make him ceremonially unclean—surely he is unclean."

1 SAMUEL 20:24-26

In one of the most ironic passages in the Bible, Saul completely looked past the fact that while he was preparing to violate one of the Ten Commandments by taking David's life—out of his own insecurity—he jumped to the conclusion that David must have done something wrong to be considered "ceremonially unclean."

If we believe we're the leader because we're the godliest, we start to see the best in ourselves and the worst in others.

This causes us to make excuses for ourselves but draw lines in the sand for others.

This causes us to think more of ourselves and less of others.

Excellent leaders, in contrast, are constantly seeking to build up their teams.

Proverbs 16:18 says, "Pride goes before destruction, and haughtiness before a fall" (NLT).

Don't miss the progression here: pride, *then* destruction. Haughtiness, *then* a fall. I've never met you, but I'd bet that "destruction" and "a fall" are nowhere on your list of top leadership goals.

Pride is one of those blind spots we can't see in the mirror. Even when we do notice it, we often give it nicknames such as "confidence" or "boldness." We need to be serious about recognizing it for what it is, because it's the very thing that got Satan kicked out of heaven. That makes it a pretty big deal.

The best way to deal with pride is to have a serious conversation with the people we lead, giving them permission to speak into our lives and not trying to defend ourselves. I've done this a number of times, and I won't lie and tell you I loved the process; however, I love what it produced in me. It's sort of like surgery: you may not enjoy being cut open, but I promise you'll enjoy having the tumor removed.

QUESTIONS TO HELP YOU LEAD IN THE MOST EXCELLENT WAY

Questions to Ask Yourself

1. Is there anyone I'm not listening to because I think I'm more intelligent than they are?
2. Is there anyone I'm not listening to because I think I'm stronger than they are?

3. Is there anyone I'm not listening to because I believe I'm godlier than they are?
4. When was the last time I admitted I made a mistake and said I was sorry in front of the people I lead?

Questions to Ask Your Team

1. What is an area of weakness in my life that I need to admit to the team?
2. What have you been trying to tell me that you feel like I haven't heard?
3. How has my pride kept us from making progress?

SUMMARY STATEMENTS

→ Don't let your pride keep you from learning from people who are smarter than you.

→ Unless you have the courage to disappoint people, you will never adequately lead them.

→ People who lead with vulnerability gain the trust of those who follow them.

→ It's okay not to feel strong; however, it's not okay to pretend you have it all together.

→ If leaders are unhealthy, then everything they lead will be unhealthy as well.

#BestWayToLead

CHAPTER 7

DOES NOT DISHONOR OTHERS

Love . . . does not dishonor others.

1 CORINTHIANS 13:4-5

I'M REALLY SORRY if you don't live in the southeastern part of the United States. That's because here we have a restaurant called Zaxby's that specializes in chicken.

I'd be letting you down if I didn't tell you their chicken fingers are *amazing* (especially if you get them with Zax Sauce). Their wings are incredible too.

If you want to go a tad healthier, their grilled chicken sandwich is one of the best grilled chicken sandwiches I've ever had (although they do smother the bread on each side with honey mustard, which might nix the health factor).

Then there are the great french fries (the crinkle-cut kind) and the sweet tea (with little bitty chunks of ice, which are easier to chomp on). But the reason you go to Zaxby's is for the chicken.

Why am I going on and on making this point?

Glad you asked!

My wife and I were walking into our local Zaxby's and were

about to order when the woman behind the register said, "Hey, I know y'all come in here a lot, so I wanted you to know before you order that we're completely out of chicken."

My wife and I laughed. The woman taking our order didn't. She looked as serious as could be, but I was sure she was playing a joke on us. So I ordered a chicken finger plate.

"Sir, I told you we're out of chicken," she said. "We don't have any wings or fingers or even anything grilled. But if you don't want any of those, I'd be glad to take your order."

"You're really out of chicken?" I asked.

"Yes, sir."

So my wife and I decided to go somewhere else. After all, if Zaxby's main thing is chicken and the main reason anyone goes there is for the chicken, then it's kind of pointless to stick around.

I've thought about that encounter a lot when it comes to leadership.

I believe one of the reasons great people join great teams, companies, and churches is because, at some level, they're expecting great leadership.

However, all too often those people find (like I did at Zaxby's) that the thing leaders should be known for (leadership) is the very thing that is missing from their menu.

This leads to our next lesson on leadership: "Love . . . does not dishonor others" (1 Corinthians 13:4-5).

If a leader doesn't have a high regard for the people on the team, the results can be tragic. This often leads to infighting and behind-the-scenes positioning, which distracts from the goal the organization is trying to accomplish.

When you think about what it means to dishonor someone, you might think of something big, like a public shaming or a cruel tweet that goes viral. But the most dishonoring actions often seem small—petty, even. In my opinion, the most dishonoring habit in the world can be summed up in one little word: *gossip*.

WHAT'S WRONG WITH GOSSIP?

Many people think gossip is just a natural part of the culture of an organization. They find all kinds of ways to rationalize it or at least call it by a different name ("venting" or "processing" or "sharing prayer requests") so they don't have to change their behavior.

But gossip isn't just a harmless break-room activity; it's something a leader has to weed out if the organization is going to be successful.

Solomon, one of the wisest leaders who ever lived, said in Proverbs 16:28, "A troublemaker plants seeds of strife; gossip separates the best of friends" (NLT).

Gossip seems to be a relative term to most people. Everyone knows what it is, and while they claim they can recognize it when they hear it, they come up short when trying to define it.

When I hear the word *gossip*, the image that pops into my mind is a girl in middle school talking to her friends between classes about what another girl wore to school that day and how ridiculous it looks. But if that's the image of gossip I carry around in my head, I'll never see it as something as serious at is—and I probably won't notice I'm guilty of it.

So if gossip isn't limited to a certain age group talking about fashion styles, what is it? Here's my definition: gossip is talking negatively about another person or situation to someone who doesn't have the authority to do anything about it.

For example, let's say you have a problem with your IT department and the most recent e-mail they sent to the staff about policies and procedures. If you decided to walk to the receptionist's desk and complain about how ridiculous the new policies were, that would be gossip.

Talking to her about the problem would be taking zero steps toward solving the problem. In fact, it would actually cause the organization to take a step back, because the conversation would result in unfocused energy and misplaced attention.

Gossip Is a Cancer

"Your mother has cancer."

Those four words changed the trajectory of my life when I was eleven years old. Over the next several months, I watched doctors aggressively try to get the cancer out of her.

They tried surgery.

They tried chemotherapy.

However, because they discovered the cancer too late and it had progressed so far, it wound up taking her life.

You don't play with cancer—it kills.

I think gossip is the cancer in most organizations (especially churches) that gets ignored and left to grow. (In many church cultures, you actually get *rewarded* for gossip, because you are seen as someone who knows what's happening and is "deeply concerned" about others.)

As leaders, we know when gossip is happening. We've heard the rumors about someone having a problem with someone else, but because we refuse to take the reins of leadership and deal with the problem, we deny that it's there or we claim that it won't have any effect on the team in the long term.

But gossip doesn't go away on its own. Don't forget—gossip is cancer, and cancer kills.

Let's go back to the illustration about the new IT policies. The wise thing would be to read them a second time, and then, if you still have a problem with them, you should walk down and talk to someone in the IT department.

One of the members of the IT department can answer your questions, provide clarification, and maybe even realize they overlooked something and fix it.

However, if you trash the IT department to the receptionist and then walk back to your desk, you've planted the idea in her mind that the IT department is full of nerds who sit around and think of ways to make people's lives miserable. You leave her with negative feelings toward an entire department in the company.

The cancer cell has been planted in her, and sooner or later someone else will stop by her desk. She may say to them, "Did you see that dumb e-mail IT sent out?"

If left unchecked, cancer always spreads.

I often tell our staff, "If you hear someone spreading gossip, call it out. Deal with it right there on the spot."

So how would this have worked in our example? The receptionist could have stopped you in the middle of your complaining and asked, "Have you spoken to the IT department about this?"

Understand this: if they gossip *to* you, then they will eventually gossip *about* you.

When you deal with the problem head on, you aren't just protecting your company's culture; you're protecting your own back as well.

As leaders, we can (and should) do something about gossip. If gossip dominates the culture of an organization, then it can't be a healthy place to work or serve.

The reality is that the cultures of our teams are either what we have created or what we have allowed. If we allow gossip to remain undealt with, it's the equivalent of leadership malpractice.

Gossip Allows Problems to Go Unresolved

After you and the receptionist have the conversation about the weirdos in IT, the problem (or the perceived problem) with the new policies and procedures is still there!

While I don't believe the primary calling on a leader's life is to walk around the office putting out fires all day, I do think the gossip issue is an important one to get under control.

Some people justify gossip by saying, "I just like to vent."

Fine, you can call it "venting," but when it involves tearing someone down when you haven't spoken to them directly, the fact remains that it's creating a culture of dishonor, whether you're involved in the gossip yourself or just allowing it to happen.

No great idea has ever taken root in someone's heart and mind because they were standing at a water cooler bashing one of their coworkers or drinking coffee in the fellowship hall criticizing a ministry volunteer.

Other people excuse their gossip by saying, "That's just the way I am."

Honestly, that may be one of the most ridiculous things I've heard anyone say.

Let's say you were walking through a parking lot and a car came flying at you out of nowhere. It ran over you, broke your leg, and then kept going.

Would you drag your busted-up leg around for the rest of your life and say, "Don't judge me—this is just the way I am. I can't help it"?

No! People would look at you like you're an idiot. They would say, "Your leg is broken. It needs to be fixed."

We all nod our heads in agreement when we're dealing with a physical problem; however, the same goes for emotional and spiritual conditions too.

When you really break it down, gossip doesn't point to the brokenness of another person; it points to the brokenness in our own lives. It shows that the posture of our hearts is bent toward dishonoring someone else rather than being brave enough to deal with the actual problem.

WAYS TO HONOR OTHERS

It's not enough to merely avoid gossiping. We also need to know how to honor others if we want to practice excellent leadership.

Deal with Confrontation Privately

One of the things I hate most about leadership is confrontation.

Even when I know it's the right thing to do.

Even when I know it's going to help the other person.

Even when I know it's going to make NewSpring a better environment to work in.

I hate it because it involves having to look another person in the eye and tell them there's something that needs to change (or that they've made a serious mistake).

Although I know it's a vital part of leadership, I just don't enjoy it. (If this is what you love about leadership, something is wrong with you!)

As a leader in a church, I'm faced with the temptation of dismissing a confrontation by saying, "I'm praying for that person and the situation" or "I'm just going to extend grace and let this go." Which is code for "I'm too weak and scared to actually lead through this intense, tough situation."

We may think we're showing love to someone by not hurting them. However, the Bible says, "An open rebuke is better than hidden love! Wounds from a sincere friend are better than many kisses from an enemy" (Proverbs 27:5-6, NLT).

If someone is working with you or for you and you know you need to confront something they've said or done, the best way to honor them is to do it privately and in person.

Not in an obscure comment during a staff meeting.

Not with a passing conversation in the hallway.

And not with a long, detailed e-mail.

Let me be clear about that last point: e-mails, texts, and social media *do not work* when it comes to confrontation. It's really easy to be bold and write things you may not say out loud; however, it's also easy to be misunderstood, as the person on the receiving end of the technological confrontation can't read your emotions or body language. Sending someone a confrontational e-mail and then walking away isn't leading—it's being passive-aggressive, which is *not* an admirable quality in any leader.

A true leader loves people enough to honor them through a private, one-on-one conversation. This is true in any leadership setting, whether you're an executive at a Fortune 500 company, the head of a small business, the pastor of a church, or a parent. If you love someone enough to confront them individually, it earns you long-term relational equity with that person.

Before we move on, there's a point that I can't leave alone. If you've ever read a leadership book or article about confrontation, chances are it said that when you confront someone, you should use the "confrontation sandwich" approach.

First, start with a compliment.

Then hit the issue you want to confront the person about.

Finally, give one more compliment, and reassure the other person as much as possible.

There are two problems with this approach.

For starters, it doesn't work. When we do this, people leave the conversation confused. They might be thinking, *Was he telling me I was doing a good job?* or *I think he really does like me.* The main point of the conversation seemed to be not the confrontation but rather making the person feel as good as possible.

I'm not giving leaders permission to be jerks here, but let's be serious: confrontation isn't supposed to feel good.

The other problem with this approach is that it gives people false expectations. Leadership experts might call this the confrontation sandwich, but I prefer to call it the "turd sandwich," and no one wants to eat one of those.

I know, I know, it's crass. But you won't forget it—I promise. Let me explain.

I love pretzel bread! Especially when it's hot and buttery.

Let's say we were going to make a sandwich out of two hot, buttery pieces of pretzel bread . . . but in the middle we placed a turd.

Question: Is the sandwich going to be awesome? After all, we did put two pieces of great bread on either side of said turd.

The answer is no!

If this is so obvious when it comes to lunch, why in the world would we think "compliment, criticism, compliment" would work? This concept must have been invented by the same people who came up with the "everyone gets a trophy for participating" idea. The danger of the turd sandwich is that it allows people to hear what they want to hear rather than what they need to hear.

If we value a person enough to talk to them one-on-one, directly, and respectfully, and then share how we believe they can do better, it's a win for everyone involved.

Confrontation is always better than condemnation—and it doesn't need to be sugarcoated to go down well.

Give Public Praise

When we have to confront someone, we should do it privately; however, when we are praising someone for a good idea or a job well done, we should be as public about it as possible.

One of the most excellent ways for leaders to earn buy-in from the people they're responsible for is public praise. When somebody hears you've been speaking highly of them when they're not present, they feel honored.

All too often, leaders talk about catching someone doing something wrong, but what if we catch them doing something right and then openly speak about it in front of as many people as possible? This is something they'll never forget. (And the higher your position as a leader, the more a public compliment will mean to them.)

A friend of mine often says, "What gets rewarded gets repeated." When we see someone going the extra mile or doing a stellar job, rewarding them with public praise shows that we value their contribution, and it encourages others in the organization to emulate what was rewarded.

Sometimes leaders don't do this because they're afraid that if they praise someone else, it will take the focus off of them as a leader. As leaders, we need to know that 99 percent of the people who work with us wonder whether they're doing a good job. For too long, I made the assumption that if I was silent, my team would know I thought they were doing great. However, my silence caused them to feel insecure and uncertain. We can't make the assumption that people know we value them and what they do; we need to discipline ourselves to give them regular feedback and encouragement.

The story of Saul and David offers a lesson about the dangers of wanting all the attention on us. If Saul had joined in with the song "Saul has killed his thousands, and David his ten thousands!"

(1 Samuel 18:7, NLT), it wouldn't have taken away from the fact that he was the king. Instead, it would have earned him buy-in with the people he led, as they would have seen that he was secure enough to recognize and reward the obvious.

Gain a Proper Perspective

One of the main reasons people are not treated with respect and honor is because our perspective gets out of whack. When we see others through the eyes of envy or self-centeredness, we can't see them for who they really are or give them the value they deserve. The proper perspective is to see people the way Jesus saw people.

Now if you think there's no place for faith in your leadership context, this may be where you'll be tempted to start skimming. If that's the case, I'd ask you to reconsider, because I really believe that if you become a leader who is more like Jesus, you'll become more like the most excellent Leader on the planet.

Jesus didn't see people as pawns to be used for His own self-promotion. In fact, He was willing to lay down His own life for them: "I am the good shepherd. The good shepherd sacrifices his life for the sheep" (John 10:11, NLT).

A call to lead is a call to serve and sacrifice. Our goal isn't to make much of ourselves; instead, we are to make much of the people we're leading. Only then will we become leaders worth following.

Jesus' willingness to believe in people, confront them, and give them second chances has always blown me away.

One of Jesus' closest disciples was Peter.

Peter was bold.

Peter was often first to speak.

Peter was usually the first to act.

However, Peter was also known for denying Jesus—not just once, but three times.

If you are the CEO of an organization and someone makes a huge mistake—one they swore they'd never make—you'd most likely have them escorted to the parking lot with a box of their stuff.

But not Jesus. After His resurrection, He sought Peter out and had a conversation with him that restored him to his job. Then Jesus allowed Peter to preach the very first sermon in church history (see John 21 and Acts 2).

Jesus didn't allow the mess in Peter's life to become the message of Peter's life.

Jesus confronted Peter privately, dealt with the situation, and then gave him an opportunity to prove himself again.

One of the verses in Scripture that has challenged me in terms of leadership focuses on the character of God:

> The LORD is merciful and compassionate,
>   slow to get angry and filled with unfailing love.
> The LORD is good to everyone.
>   He showers compassion on all his creation.
> PSALM 145:8-9, NLT

Contrary to what the world will tell you, excellent leaders are the ones who are full of mercy and compassion.

QUESTIONS TO HELP YOU LEAD IN THE MOST EXCELLENT WAY

Questions to Ask Yourself

1. Do I gossip about the people I lead or the people who lead me? Do I allow gossip to taint the environment I lead in?

2. Who is one person I need to confront privately this week? Who is one person I need to praise publicly?

Questions to Ask Your Team

1. Would you describe me as being full of compassion or full of condemnation? Why?
2. What can we do to create a culture of honoring others in our organization?

SUMMARY STATEMENTS

→   If people gossip *to* you, then they will eventually gossip *about* you.

→   Gossip doesn't point to the brokenness of another person; it points to the brokenness in our own lives.

→   A true leader loves people enough to confront them in a private, one-on-one conversation.

→   A call to lead is a call to serve and sacrifice.

→   Jesus was willing to believe in people, confront them, and give them a second chance.

#BestWayToLead

CHAPTER 8

NOT SELF-SEEKING

Love . . . is not self-seeking.
1 CORINTHIANS 13:4-5

I'M NOT A FOOD SHARER.

I do not like food sharers.

I get angry if someone reaches over and takes food off my plate—angry enough to stab their hand with a fork.

After all, it's my food.

When I'm out to dinner with someone and they say, "Hey, I've never tried that" ("that" being what is on my plate), my response to them is always, "You'll have to get that one day."

No, you can't have "just a few" of my fries—I'd rather buy you your own order of fries than give you three or four of mine.

As passionate as I am about not sharing the entrée portion of my meal, I'm even more extreme in my food-sharing condemnation when it comes to dessert.

I love dessert. Sometimes I won't even pay attention to a meal I'm eating, because I'm so obsessed with the dessert coming at the end of it.

This is especially true when it comes to one of my favorite desserts in the world: ice cream.

I could eat tubs of ice cream every day for the rest of my life. I know this wouldn't be healthy, but at least I would die happy!

Now that you know this about me, I want to take you behind the scenes to one of the most intense arguments my wife, Lucretia, and I have ever had.

We were meeting some friends at a local ice cream spot, and when we pulled up, Lucretia told me she wasn't really that hungry. She said she thought it would be best if we shared something.

Immediately I was on the defense. I told her it was okay not to finish the dessert she ordered; however, she assured me she just wanted "a bite or two" of whatever I was going to get.

I calmed down a little; after all, if she just wanted a bite or two, then I would be okay.

So I ordered the largest hot-fudge brownie they had and asked them to cover it with ice cream and whipped cream. Then I asked for two spoons. This shocked the friends we were with because they knew about my dessert obsession. One of them actually said, "I just about peed my pants when I heard you ask for two spoons. I don't think I have ever seen you share a dessert."

I set the massive dessert down on the table and became engaged in the conversation around the table. My mistake was that I completely lost focus on the dessert in front of me.

After a few minutes, I looked down and saw that Lucretia's "few bites" had turned into half of the brownie sundae. And there was no indication that she was slowing down.

Did I mention she was pregnant?

At this point I had a choice. I could simply let the issue go unaddressed, or I could call her out in front of everyone.

I chose the latter. "Dang, woman—slow down! You're eating way more than you said you would!"

Side note: It's never a good idea to let these words come out of your mouth. *Ever!*

Needless to say, there was some instant tension in the air.

But I was convinced I was in the right; after all, she said she only wanted a few bites. She'd never eaten more than half of any dessert we'd shared in the past.

When we got back in the car, we seriously had an argument over the whole thing. It wasn't until later that evening, when I was sitting on the living room couch reflecting on what had happened, that I thought, *All of this could have been avoided if I hadn't been so selfish.*

So many problems in leadership can be boiled down to selfishness, whether on our part or on the part of our team members.

The next piece of leadership advice in 1 Corinthians 13 is that "love . . . is not self-seeking" (verses 4-5).

We're self-seeking when we pursue what's best for us and no one else, when we lose sight of people and end up manipulating them. Self-seeking happens when we buy in to the idea that life is all about getting ahead.

Self-seeking people are quick to throw others under the bus but slow to accept any responsibility or blame.

They're the people who won't allow any idea except their own to be the most talked about and praised.

They're the people who talk to you not because they care about you but because they're trying to get something from you.

No one respects leaders like this. My question is, if these are the kind of people we hate working with, why would we allow ourselves to act this way?

I've found some tough questions about guarding against selfishness in Isaiah 49. Here are four we'd be wise to ask ourselves on a regular basis to keep our egos in check.

HOW MUCH TIME DO YOU SPEND LISTENING TO GOD?

Every leader has great ideas.

Every leadership team has great ideas.

The Internet is full of leadership articles, videos, and quotes that we can all take to heart and learn from.

However, in my own leadership, I've discovered that if I don't intentionally take time to focus on listening to what God wants, I will become a self-seeking leader who wants what's best for me rather than what's best for the team.

God wants nothing but the absolute best for our lives, and I believe people in any area of leadership will improve their lives if they take the time to listen to what He has to say.

If a new leader came to me asking how to lead well, the best advice I could give them is "Listen to Jesus, and do what He says."

I'm sure you'd expect me to say this—after all, I'm a pastor.

But this advice isn't just for pastors. I believe listening to God leads to success whether you're a pastor, a small-business owner, a doctor, a politician, a dad, a mom, or someone who has a nine-to-five job that just pays the bills.

God wants the absolute best for our lives, but we'll only know what that is if we spend time finding out what He has to say.

Isaiah 49:1 says, "*Listen* to me, all you in distant lands! *Pay attention*, you who are far away! The LORD *called me* before my birth; from within the womb he *called me* by name" (NLT, emphasis added). In this one verse, we see four separate references to listening to God.

In the past fifteen years of leadership, I've had to make some incredibly difficult decisions—some that directly impacted the livelihood of a number of people, some that had million-dollar price tags attached to them, and some that kept me up at night thinking about various what-if scenarios.

All too often, I freak myself out because I falsely assume I'm alone in this roller coaster of leadership.

But then, as He always does, God reminds me that He's with me and that He hasn't called me to walk this journey on my own.

Self-seeking people don't seek God because, at the end of the day, they don't want to share the credit for their successes with anyone.

But by now I know that every leadership decision I've made that has produced any type of good fruit has been the result not of my brilliance but of God's goodness.

Let's dive back into David's story again. Think about all the times he was all alone in the desert with the sheep. We know from the psalms he wrote that he spent lots of time talking to and listening to God. And as he went through various challenges in his life, he asked God for advice.

When the Philistines heard that David had been anointed king of Israel, they mobilized all their forces to capture him. But David was told they were coming, so he went into the stronghold. The Philistines arrived and spread out across the valley of Rephaim. So David asked the LORD, "Should I go out to fight the Philistines? Will you hand them over to me?"

The LORD replied to David, "Yes, go ahead. I will certainly hand them over to you."

So David went to Baal-perazim and defeated the Philistines there. "The LORD did it!" David exclaimed. "He burst through my enemies like a raging flood!" So he named that place Baal-perazim (which means "the Lord

who bursts through"). The Philistines had abandoned
their idols there, so David and his men confiscated them.

2 SAMUEL 5:17-21 (NLT)

Don't you love this? David, a man who had fought plenty of
battles by this point, was facing a decision about whether or not
to go to war with his enemies. He knew how to fight. He knew
all about military strategy and precision. He could have huddled
with his commanders and come up with a brilliant battle plan that
would have sent the bad guys running for their lives.

But instead he paused, refusing to rely on his experience, and
humbly asked God what He wanted.

And God answered.

Then, right after David faced an intense situation, he was faced
almost immediately with a similar challenge.

After a while the Philistines returned and again spread
out across the valley of Rephaim. And *again David asked
the Lord what to do*. "Do not attack them straight on,"
the Lord replied. "Instead, circle around behind and
attack them near the poplar trees. When you hear a
sound like marching feet in the tops of the poplar trees,
be on the alert! That will be the signal that the Lord is
moving ahead of you to strike down the Philistine army."
So *David did what the Lord commanded*, and he struck
down the Philistines all the way from Gibeon to Gezer.

2 SAMUEL 5:22-25, NLT (EMPHASIS ADDED)

What did David do? He didn't rely on what he did the last
time; he didn't make assumptions about the current plans based

on what had worked in the past; he didn't claim he had everything figured out.

Once again, he asked God what to do. And once again, God answered. David's life serves as proof that success is tied to listening to God and doing what He says.

Listening to God and doing what He says is not just for people in ministry; it's for everyone—from soldiers like David to executives at secular corporations. If you're a CEO, God wants you to be the best CEO you can be. If you're a small-business owner, God wants you to be the best small-business owner you can be. If you lead a Bible study in your kitchen, God wants you to be the best Bible study leader you can be.

Leaning into God keeps us humble and reminds us that what we're doing—and who we're doing it for—is much greater than any self-seeking desires we may be tempted to follow and allow to dominate our lives.

ARE YOU MORE CONCERNED ABOUT BEING DISCOVERED OR BEING DEVELOPED?

Wrong turns can cost us a great deal of time.

I remember going to visit a friend in Oklahoma and taking a wrong turn on my way to his house. That wrong turn led me onto a highway where I had to drive eighteen miles before I could find a place to turn around and begin heading in the right direction.

When someone wants to be discovered more than they want to be developed, they've taken a wrong turn in their leadership.

This happens often with young leaders. They're full of vision and dreams and ideas, and they don't understand that time is one of the greatest leadership tools God ever created.

But this can happen with older leaders as well. It's easy for them to get caught up in comparison, seeing how they measure up against other businesses, movements, or churches until they become jealous of the attention other people are receiving.

Isaiah 49:2 says, "He made my words of judgment as sharp as a sword. *He has hidden me in the shadow of his hand.* I am like a sharp arrow in his quiver" (NLT, emphasis added).

One of the greatest gifts God can give us is to hide us while He shapes us.

One of the reasons He does this, I believe, is because He most often develops our character when no one else is looking.

People who are self-seeking tend to compromise their character for the right opportunity. And character isn't just a peripheral concept in leadership development. It's the essential quality that enables us to lead in the most excellent way for the long term.

Our success won't be determined by our position on an org chart but rather by how well we are able to work with others—and this is the result of having strong character.

In the early days when I was in youth ministry, I began serving part-time at a church that had around fifteen students. I remember the frustration of being in such a small place with a budget that was so limited and circumstances that were less than ideal. However, the Lord used that place to develop me into a leader who would be able to handle much more than I could have imagined at the time. I needed to develop as a leader in behind-the-scenes ways before I'd be ready for the places God would call me to in the future.

If you're not receiving the attention you think you deserve, don't consider yourself cursed; consider yourself blessed. Allow God to hide you until He has helped you work past the desire for self-promotion in your leadership position.

When our character has been developed and our desires are more about God and others than about being recognized, we are finally in a position to accomplish the goals God has in mind for us.

ARE YOU BELIEVING ANY LIES?

No one has lied to you, hurt you, or deceived you more than you've done those things to yourself.

I remember sitting down with a friend and telling him my thought process. He said, "If you spoke to other people the way you speak to yourself, you'd have zero friends."

In Isaiah, we see an example of how even God's most famous prophets can believe lies about their work:

> [The Lord] said to me, "You are my servant, Israel,
>   and you will bring me glory."
>
> I replied, "*But my work seems so useless!*
>   I have spent my strength for nothing and *to no purpose.*
> Yet I leave it all in the Lord's hand;
>   I will trust God for my reward."
>
> And now the Lord speaks—
>   the one who formed me in my mother's womb to be his
>   servant,
>   who commissioned me to bring Israel back to him.
> The Lord has honored me,
>   and my God has given me strength.

ISAIAH 49:3-5, NLT (EMPHASIS ADDED)

Isaiah is saying here that he's discouraged, that his work has been useless, and that he has been wasting his time because what he's doing has no purpose.

Have you ever felt like that?

One of the biggest battles a leader has to deal with is the battle against discouragement.

All of us, no matter what career or position we have, are going to have bad days.

Some of us are going to have bad seasons.

And the temptation during these times is to feed ourselves an endless supply of negative talk.

When self-seeking leaders don't see progress, one temptation they face is to externalize the disappointment and point to the faults of others. Or they might fall into the trap of internalizing all that has gone wrong and blame themselves for all their "dumb decisions." They make their successes all about themselves, but they also make their flops all about themselves.

The last thing self-seeking leaders do in this situation is ask for help, because they're afraid doing so will make them look bad.

However, I've discovered that the only way to get rid of the negative self-talk and lies that fly into my mind is to be open with the people I work with. I need them to tell me the truth whenever I'm buying into something that isn't true.

It can be terrifying to open up to people enough to let them see the lies we're believing. It's tempting to hold it all in; after all, we don't want people to think we're crazy!

But I've discovered firsthand that when I'm open about the lies I'm battling, the people I'm leading don't disrespect me as a result; rather, they respect me *more*. My vulnerability also allows them to be more open about the lies they've been believing about themselves.

Leaders set the tone. And if we want honesty and transparency to dominate our culture, we have to be the ones not only to declare those things as values in our organization but also to live them out.

ARE YOU TAKING RISKS OR PLAYING IT SAFE?

It was early 2007, and I had to make a leadership decision that, at the time, was the biggest leadership challenge I'd faced in my entire life.

Our church had been portable for around six years. Since we rented a building on Sunday mornings, we had to set up every Sunday around five in the morning and then pack everything back into trucks and trailers at the end of the day.

Then, in February of 2006, we moved into a permanent facility. We were excited to have a home base, and we thought we'd be able to cruise for two or three years.

However, within eight months of the move, our attendance doubled, going from four thousand each weekend to more than eight thousand.

We suddenly had some important decisions to make.

We couldn't turn around and build a second building—we didn't have the land or the cash.

We were already out of space in our children's area, as we'd underestimated the square footage we'd need to accommodate the kids who showed up every Sunday.

Our student ministry was growing so rapidly that every two or three months, the middle school and high school students outgrew any facility we rented for them to meet in.

We had a number of people coming each week from Greenville, South Carolina (about thirty minutes away). That group said they couldn't convince their unchurched friends to attend with them in Anderson, but if there were a NewSpring campus in Greenville, they thought it would be successful.

So the leaders of our church began meeting to see if we could accomplish all these things at once: expanding our existing children's space, building a new student ministry center, and starting our first multisite campus in Greenville. The total price tag came to $20 million.

The first time I heard that dollar amount, my heart sank into my stomach. This would take work—a lot of work. We'd have to begin a capital campaign and try to raise the funds. I'd have to spend countless hours meeting with people and casting a compelling vision. Nothing like this had ever been attempted by any church in our area.

I was in over my head—and I knew it.

During the meeting when we had to make the final decision about whether we'd launch the $20-million initiative, I had to call a time-out and tell the other leaders around the table I needed to go home for the day because I just couldn't get clarity on what I was supposed to do.

When I walked into the house, Lucretia took one look at me and said, "What's wrong?"

I told her about everything I was wrestling with and explained the $20-million price tag. "I just don't know if this is even possible," I said.

Then she said something I'll never forget.

She reminded me about a move our church had wrestled through when we were about a year and a half old. We had to go from one location to another, and the total cost of the move was about $46,000.

The people in our church gave as sacrificially as they could, and we raised around $26,000, but we still needed $20,000, or the move simply was not going to happen.

After much negotiating with banks and trying to find a bank crazy enough to loan a start-up church $20,000, I finally found one, and one of the church leaders and I signed a personal note saying that if the church couldn't pay, we would.

Was I nervous? I didn't sleep for three weeks! But sure enough, I saw God do amazing things, and the $20,000 was paid off early.

With this in mind, Lucretia asked me, "Why in the world would you trust God for $20,000 but not trust Him for $20 million? Isn't He able to do it?"

Oh, snap!

At that moment, the switch flipped in my mind, and I made the decision that we were going to move forward with the projects that had been put before us.

As I look back on that incident now, I realize I'd allowed a self-seeking attitude to creep into my thought patterns and hold me back from taking God-sized risks.

I liked the idea of not having to work as hard for a while.

I liked the idea of putting the organization I was leading on cruise control.

I liked the idea of "playing it safe" and enjoying a season of calm in my life.

I wanted what was best for me—but not what was best for the people I was there to serve.

Haven't we all battled this desire to coast at some point? We reach a stage in our leadership where we cease to focus on growth and instead concentrate on maintaining the status quo.

When this happens, we'd be wise to look at what God says to Isaiah in this passage: "You will do more than restore the people of Israel to me. I will make you a light to the Gentiles, and you will bring my salvation to the ends of the earth" (Isaiah 49:6, NLT).

The symbolism in this verse is amazing.

Isaiah had in mind that this message would be a light to the Jewish nation, but God's vision was for this message to be a light to the entire world.

Isaiah had a limited view of what God wanted.

One of the worst things we can do as leaders is subject the people we're responsible to lead to our small, safe ideas.

I believe God always wants more for us than we want for ourselves.

I believe He wants our churches to be full of people who are filled with life and hope and are contagious in the communities they're planted in.

I believe He wants more with your business or company.

I believe He wants more with your family.

Yes, God gets glory when a church or business or ministry grows in numbers; however, I would argue He gets as much (if not more) glory when a person who is unashamed of their faith leans into Him, seeks to grow, refuses to believe lies about themselves, and then dreams big to fulfill the vision God has in store for them.

If God is as big as the Bible says He is and He can do as much as the Bible says He can do, then why, when we're making our plans with Him, would we make our plans small, safe, and predictable?

I believe one of the best questions a leader in any field can ask of God when they experience success is "What now, Lord?"

I don't think the One who literally walked through hell will lead us to safe and predictable places.

When He says, "Go," He has a plan—one that will prosper us, not harm us; one that will give us hope and a future; one that will allow us to put our self-seeking tendencies aside and love God and people way more than we love our own comfort.

Would you seek marriage advice from the person who has blown through three marriages?

Would you seek cooking advice from someone who can't even open a can of Chef Boyardee?

If not, then why in the world would you surrender your thoughts and emotions to someone online who has never accomplished anything relevant to your situation?

When it comes to leadership, listen to the people who have actually led something.

Anyone can tell you what you did wrong after you made the business deal or delivered the sermon or disciplined your child. However, the person who is constantly pointing out your flaws and tearing apart everything you do is not worth the emotional energy you're surrendering to them.

Coaches Handle Things Privately; Critics Go Public

Watching coaches make corrections during the course of the game has been eye opening for me. When they approach the player, they pull him off to the side and deal with the issue man-to-man.

I've never seen a great coach take control of the PA system and tell the entire crowd about the player's problem, publicly tearing his performance or character to pieces. That type of behavior would be shocking at a sporting event, but it seems to be acceptable in certain leadership arenas.

That may be because critics are often seeking the platform for themselves. Their goal isn't to sincerely address the issue and work toward a resolution; rather, they want to be recognized.

I've become painfully aware of this reality over the past several years because, on occasion, I've sat down and talked with people who were seeking to tear me apart, along with the church I lead.

I asked to meet with them face-to-face because I sincerely thought I could explain my heart and my intentions to them, and that by doing so I'd be able to change their minds about me.

So I asked these critics to share the reasons for their concerns. Every single time, with only one exception, they refused an individual meeting and instead requested a public forum for debate. This confused me at first until I realized that critics want to make a point, while coaches want to make a difference.

Coaches Love You through a Disagreement; Critics Hate You No Matter What

I've had a few instances in my life when godly men and women have confronted me on an issue, and after a lot of thought, discussion, and prayer, we decided to agree to disagree.

These situations have been painful for me because I'm committed to honoring the coaches God has placed in my life; however, there are some issues that godly people never see eye-to-eye on—even when it comes to those closest to you.

The difference between disagreements with coaches and disagreements with critics is that even when you land in different places, coaches still love you.

After a sermon I gave at my church, someone I respect pulled me aside and told me he disagreed with some of the content I'd delivered in the message. He talked to me one-on-one, face-to-face, and he did so with honor and respect. Eventually we came to the conclusion that we saw the issue differently. However, our love and respect for each other actually increased through the process.

Critics rarely take this stance. They don't know you. They haven't rejoiced with you or wept with you. They've never seen you struggle through a situation. They've never witnessed what you do behind the scenes. They don't know about the sleepless nights you've experienced as the result of what you really love to do.

Critics just hate.

And you do yourself (and the people you lead) zero good if you allow these negative voices to anger you and distract you from what you're supposed to be doing.

Coaches Should Be Listened To; Critics Should Be Ignored

I've had people ask me, now that the church I lead has grown into something beyond what I could have imagined, whether I still need people to speak into my life.

My response is always the same: "I've never needed great coaches around me more than I do right now!"

We will never reach the place in our leadership where we don't need honest feedback, even when it's difficult to hear.

Correction doesn't feel good in the moment; however, as I look back over my life at the coaches who have loved me enough to correct me, I feel thankful that these men and women could speak honestly to me—even if what they were telling me wasn't what I wanted to hear.

We can't attain success in leadership by giving everyone who has an opinion emotional access to our lives. If we do, we'll become easily angered, bitter, cynical leaders who don't trust anyone.

When I was dealing with the online battle, I knew I needed to take drastic steps to get my anger under control, so I called a coach to talk through this with me.

After I explained the situation, he said, "How many times a day are you going to the website to see what this person is saying about you?"

"About twenty," I replied.

I'll never forget what he said next.

"Perry, criticism on the Internet is like verbal pornography. You know you shouldn't look at it, but somehow you keep going back there, reading it over and over again, hoping things will change."

Then he said, "That's not great leadership. You're allowing people who don't even know you to hijack your emotions and decisions. You can't control what they're saying, but you can control how much attention you pay to it."

Criticism is something every leader faces at some point. We can't control what people say to us; the only thing we can control is how we will respond.

The best way to prevent anger from taking over is to set up coaches in our lives, listen to what they say, and ignore everyone else.

QUESTIONS TO HELP YOU LEAD IN THE MOST EXCELLENT WAY

Questions to Ask Yourself

1. Is there any decision I'm afraid to make because I'm worried about what others will think of it?
2. What coaches in my life have license to tell me what I need to hear?

Questions to Ask Your Team

1. Do we as a team allow critical people to hijack the majority of our time and thoughts?
2. Who are we listening to most as a team? Are these people coaches or critics?

SUMMARY STATEMENTS

→ Criticism has the potential to ignite a fire that consumes you and takes control of your emotions.

→ If you're going to accomplish anything significant as a leader, you need to listen to your coaches, not your critics.

→ Don't allow the voices of those who know you the least to shape you the most.

→ Critics want to make a point, while coaches want to make a difference.

→ Don't allow people who don't even know you to hijack your emotions and decisions.

#BestWayToLead

CHAPTER 10

KEEPS NO RECORD OF WRONGS

Love . . . keeps no record of wrongs.
I CORINTHIANS 13:4-5

CHANCES ARE YOU DON'T REMEMBER where you were on March 23, 2009, but it's a date I'll never forget.

I distinctly remember driving down the road and hearing on the radio that the company BI-LO (a chain of grocery stores in the southeastern part of the United States) was declaring bankruptcy.

It was an announcement I didn't think a whole lot about at the time; however, within the next three months, that news was forever sealed in my brain. That was the day I should have received an award for being the most idiotic leader in the world.

But first let me catch you up on the story.

In 2006 our church built a 2,500-seat auditorium in Anderson, South Carolina. We were sure that would be adequate for the next several years. We moved into the new building in February of that year, and by October we were holding three services every weekend, all at capacity.

We were scratching our heads, wondering what in the world to do. None of us had seen this coming.

Then several pieces came together at the same time that caused us to believe we were stepping into the perfect story. In reality, however, it was the perfect storm.

The first thing that seized our attention was the fact that a few churches were embracing a new style of church called "multisite." According to this model, everything at a campus is live except the message, which is supplied via video from a broadcast campus. We spent some time studying this idea, and eventually we completely embraced it because we believed it would help us in our goal of reaching more people.

The second piece of information that was brought to our attention was that we had a significant number of people from Greenville attending our church. Greenville is larger than Anderson, and it's about twenty to thirty minutes away. We had one thousand or so families attending from this city; the only real complaint they had was that it was nearly impossible for them to convince their unchurched family members and friends to attend, since it was so far away.

After searching for a facility and agreeing to the lease terms, we decided to begin a campus in Greenville. We spent about $4 million getting it retrofitted and ready to serve as a church. In July 2008, we held our first service there, with 1,710 people in attendance. We just knew we were on the way to seeing more success than we could imagine.

Except for one little detail.

When we signed the lease agreement, it was actually a sublease. BI-LO had originally leased the building for a set amount from a business in Greenville and, after shutting down the store, allowed our church to step in and sublease the building for half the amount they were paying for it.

It was a great deal—until they went bankrupt, which nullified any subleases they'd agreed to.

This was the first multisite facility we had launched. None of us on the leadership team knew much about these types of agreements, and in retrospect, I can see that the right decision would have been to hire a lawyer and get them to read over the lease agreement from the very beginning.

But come on, who has time (or money) for lawyers?

Before we signed the lease, I asked our CFO if he'd read over the contract, and he said he had. He was the only person on our leadership team with any real estate experience, and he said that it looked good but it might be worthwhile to hire someone else to review it since he didn't know specifically what to look for.

At that moment I made the decision to move forward; after all, eternity is long and hell is hot! We didn't have time to dot *i*'s, cross *t*'s, and deal with a bunch of legal details.

The campus exploded, and by Christmas of that year, we were up to more than three thousand people. The new year began with a bang for the new facility, and we kept adding services.

Now, back to the bankruptcy.

Our CFO received a phone call from the business BI-LO was leasing from and informed us that since BI-LO had declared bankruptcy, we were now expected to pay what they'd been paying as well, which meant doubling our rent.

When I heard the news, I hit the roof. There was no way they could do this to us! We had an agreement! We'd signed a document! At this point we decided to seek legal counsel. Unfortunately, we were told that the terms were clearly spelled out in the agreement: if for some reason BI-LO ever declared bankruptcy, any subleases they had signed would be null and void.

Over the next few days, we cried and prayed and fumed. We desperately wanted to keep meeting in Greenville; however, we simply weren't able to afford the astronomical rent.

Finally, we had no choice but to walk away from the building we'd spent more than $4 million on while getting it ready to serve as a church site. We'd occupied the facility for less than a year.

The Greenville campus was moved to a portable location, and we essentially had to launch the church all over again.

It was painful, but we managed to pull through this challenge as a team. As I look back on that experience now, I believe one of the reasons we were able to navigate it and move forward was because no one tried to blame anyone else for the mess-up. And we didn't allow it to define us as we moved forward.

We could have held the CFO accountable. After all, he told our entire leadership team he'd read the contract and didn't see anything wrong with it. In return, he could have held my feet to the fire by reminding me he'd suggested that we hire an attorney.

The campus pastor and staff in Greenville could have held a grudge against the leadership team of our church for not setting them up for success.

The church members could have turned their backs on the leaders because we hadn't ensured that the money they gave wouldn't go down the drain.

However, no one pointed fingers like that.

People communicated trust as clearly and as quickly as possible.

No one was fired.

No one was demoted.

The next time we had to negotiate a deal, we didn't say, "Well, so-and-so really screwed it up last time. . . ."

We knew we'd made a mistake, and we learned from it and then moved on.

We didn't throw anyone's shortcomings in their faces, because excellent leaders don't keep track of wrongs.

"Love . . . keeps no record of wrongs" (1 Corinthians 13:4-5).

There are way too many people who wake up paranoid every morning, afraid they're just one mistake away from the wrath of the people in charge. They wonder if today will be the day they'll mess up a client relationship or fail to close a deal or bomb their talk to the board, and it will be game over for them.

Insecure leaders tend to use someone on the team (often a younger member) to make a point to everyone else about what not to do. And in some environments, these "charges" never get dropped. If you royally messed up a decade ago, people are still talking about it to this day. This kind of record keeping creates a culture of fear. It discourages people from taking risks and striving to do better because they're afraid it might cost them their jobs.

OUR OPTIONS FOR DEALING WITH MISTAKES

When someone we lead makes an honest mistake, we have three options.

We Can Scream

When leaders lose their temper and go off on someone for messing up, they create a culture of fear. In this kind of environment, people rarely live up to their potential, and it's almost impossible for a team to meet its goals. Leaders who constantly play the yelling card end up revealing more about their own shortcomings than those of the person they're screaming at. They're showing a serious lack of self-control, and leaders who lack self-control always end up leading the team into chaos and dysfunction.

We Can Go Silent

Some leaders stop talking to the individual who made the mistake. Instead of addressing the issue head-on, they do everything they can to avoid the offender.

Unfortunately, this was the way I used to cope with people who made mistakes. I wouldn't return their calls or e-mails, and I wouldn't speak to them when I saw them. I wanted them to suffer because of how badly they'd screwed up.

This behavior from a leader creates a culture of manipulation and uncertainty. If leaders don't deal with a situation, people aren't able to move on and learn from their mistakes, and eventually trust erodes between the leader and the team.

Thankfully I discovered that this style of leadership wasn't helping our team move forward; it was holding us back and placing us under a cloud of doubt. I found that it was much healthier (for them and for me) to confront the situation in a spirit of honesty and love.

We Can Learn

No matter what kind of organization or team you're part of, making a mistake can be an opportunity to learn. I can honestly say that some of the best leadership lessons I've learned have come as the result of my own stupidity, carelessness, and immaturity.

When a leader's first reaction to someone who has made a mistake is "Let's see what we can learn from this" as opposed to "Go clean out your office," there's so much more relational equity and buy-in from the entire team.

When someone makes a mistake, it's not just an opportunity for that person to learn; it's also an opportunity for us to learn as leaders. The situation provides an opening for us to investigate our own motives in leadership.

One of the most powerful questions to ask ourselves when one of our people has messed up is "What do I want for this person as a result of what just happened?"

If we want to use the situation to prove a point to everyone else, then we are using people.

If we want to create fear in the team, then we are manipulating people.

If we want to use this mistake as an excuse to bring back all the stupid things that person has ever done, then we are making them look worse so we can look better.

But if we want to produce a sense of security and honesty in the team, then we are leading people well.

WHEN LEADERS ARE THEIR OWN WORST ENEMY

Let's take a look at Saul and David again to see these principles in action.

Saul thought he'd been wronged by David. The people were giving accolades to David—accolades Saul thought he deserved himself. Saul couldn't let go of that perceived wrong, and this eventually led him to undermine his own leadership.

Tearing Your People Down

Saul's record keeping caused him to tear David down instead of building him up. Instead of having a vulnerable conversation with David and attempting to find a way to leverage David's influence and potential for the greater good, Saul decided to shatter one of the Ten Commandments and try to kill him.

When leaders seek to tear people down rather than build them up, there's a serious problem. A call to lead is actually a call to serve, and we don't serve people well when we scream at them or give them the silent treatment. Real leaders seek to understand why the person on their team made a particular decision—and then they help them comprehend a different way of thinking, if needed.

What type of leadership environment did Saul create around him? It seems clear that he was a "screamer." I imagine that if someone in his court had an idea that was a bit different from his own (or even if it was something Saul wished he'd come up with himself), Saul would have shut it down. And after a while, people probably stopped coming to Saul with their ideas, because doing so would cause Saul to feel threatened.

Whether we like it or not, the tone the leader sets eventually becomes the tone of the entire organization.

Secure leaders create secure environments.

Angry leaders create angry environments.

And leaders who love others create environments where people really do love and care about one another—which is one of the most attractive environments in the world.

Focusing on Things That Aren't Important

Saul's number-one job was to lead Israel. I'm sure there were plenty of details that needed his attention—everything from the military to trade decisions to the economy.

However, because of Saul's obsession with David, he was distracted from doing what he was supposed to do as he tried to destroy a young man who had never sought to bring him any harm.

It's possible to become so obsessed with what people are doing wrong that we lose sight of all they're doing right.

Saul forgot that David had defeated Goliath.

Saul forgot that David had won every battle he was sent into.

Saul forgot that David had been completely loyal to him.

chosen him." So David restrained his men and did not let them kill Saul.

1 SAMUEL 24:5-7

Conviction over Convenience

David chose the convictions in his heart over the conveniences in his life.

The best leaders don't keep a record of wrongs, and David was no exception. Instead of crushing his enemy, David chose compassion. This seems like a dangerous decision at first; however, David wasn't about in-the-moment leadership. He knew that effective leadership is about the long haul—which meant that the way he treated people, even his enemies, would have an effect on the people who were under his care.

When someone isn't doing a great job, it seems easier to just fire them or, to use the more politically correct phrase, "launch them into a new career opportunity."

David was an excellent leader, and he valued people more than a title. As a result, he was able to make a wise decision for the long term—one that ended up propelling his leadership forward. If David had killed Saul on the spot, it probably would have been temporarily effective but ultimately shortsighted. The Old Testament records a number of kings who were assassinated by rebel groups. More often than not, this type of overthrow inevitably led to national instability and another assassination. Leadership that's rooted in bitterness, anger, and revenge never produces a desirable environment over the long term.

In that critical moment, David was able to see Saul as a human being. He decided to trust God more than he trusted himself.

As leaders, we are responsible for the way we lead those who serve with us. In my role, I'm personally responsible for more than four hundred employees, and I have a picture of every single one of them in my office. Whenever I have to make a decision about one of the people on my team, I listen to the people around me. I'm also committed to considering each person and their unique situation.

Devotion over Desires

David also chose devotion to the process over his personal desires. He didn't allow himself to become obsessed over how Saul had wronged him; instead, he kept his eyes on God's bigger plan.

Did David want to be king? Absolutely!

Did David enjoy running for his life? Nope!

Do you think he would have liked to live in a palace instead of a cave? I know royal living would appeal more to me!

However, David knew that if he allowed his personal desires to take over, it would cost the king his life—and it would cost David a great legacy.

It's not wrong to want to get ahead as a leader; however, when we get ahead because we stepped on other people, that's not success but short-term gain in exchange for our reputations.

CREATING A CULTURE FREE FROM RECORD KEEPING

When it comes to dealing with people, I try to ask myself four questions to ensure that I'm not keeping a record of my team's wrongs.

Is This a Consistent Issue?

At this point you may be wondering, *If leaders don't keep a record of wrongs, does that mean I'm never allowed to confront someone about an issue with their work?*

For example, let's say you have a policy that people are supposed to be at work at nine in the morning.

Then you have Jim.

Jim is a great guy who does a good job; however, he just can't seem to make it to the office on time.

In this scenario, does "love keeps no record of wrongs" mean you can never chat with Jim about the importance of getting to work on time?

Not at all!

The ideology behind not keeping a record applies to the heart behind the confrontation. If a person consistently makes the same mistake or doesn't meet the expectations of an organization, it's the responsibility of the leader to have a difficult conversation.

Doing so is not keeping a record of wrongs; in fact, it goes a long way in preventing resentment from building in your heart over those wrongs.

If you fail to have a difficult conversation when someone is not meeting standards, you will begin to draw some conclusions regarding their performance. Every time they make a mistake, your mind will go back to all the times in the past when they haven't met expectations.

So in Jim's case, every time you see him walk in late, your anger and resentment grow—little by little at first, until one day you fly at Jim for being late, leaving him confused and frustrated. After all, if it was such a big deal, why are you just now getting around to saying something about it?

If the problem is consistent, it demands a conversation. Things don't just get better on their own.

There's also the plus side to confrontation: maybe a conversation with Jim will result in his becoming more disciplined and gaining an understanding for why showing up on time is a value.

And maybe a conversation with Jim will open up new information for you as a leader. Let's say that Jim's wife has always taken the kids to school; however, she's been really sick for the past three months and hasn't been able to do so. Jim isn't slacking off—he's been trying to take care of his family, and he didn't think it was that big of a deal to be a little late.

Is This a Competence Issue?

I got two Cs in college; the rest were As and Bs.

Both Cs were in science classes—I've never been good at science. The only time I enjoyed science class was when my tenth-grade biology teacher, Mrs. Fazone, informed us as we were dissecting rats that if we were to take out a rat's intestines, they would stretch across the entire room—and then she walked out!

What was I to do? I was a natural skeptic, and this was something I had a hard time believing. So I handed my lab partner one end of the rat's insides and walked across the room with the other to see if she was correct.

She was! And she came back into the room at the exact point that my lab partner and I began to swing the insides of the poor rat around like a jump rope.

That's the only fond memory I have of anything relating to science class.

My Cs in college were a competence issue, not an effort issue. I just didn't get biology. If my dream in life had been to become a doctor, I think I'd still be in college trying to figure out what on earth a zygote is.

People may have the greatest intentions in the world but lack the competence to do the job they've been tasked with. When leaders face this situation, they must decide whether the person can be taught a specific set of skills or whether the particular job is not a good fit for them.

I really want to believe in people and give them the benefit of the doubt, so it's particularly challenging for me to deal with people who simply aren't able to do the task before them. But one of the marks of being a good leader is knowing when to make the call on someone's incompetence.

One thing that has helped me in this area has been to recognize that if people don't have the competence to do one thing, that doesn't mean they aren't gifted in other areas.

Thankfully, my biology professor in college didn't take me to the dean and demand that I be thrown out because I didn't understand his class. He got that everyone in the world isn't supposed to be a scientist. (Thank God!)

If you have someone on your team who doesn't have the competence to do their job well and you refuse to have a conversation with them about it, it will place them (and you) in a state of perpetual frustration, because both of you know they're doing a bad job. And while it might seem "nice" to overlook the problem, it's actually not loving that person well. Rather, it's being selfish because you know that having a difficult conversation with them might be incredibly uncomfortable and inconvenient.

If you want to be a leader people are excited to work with and give their best for, it's vital that you use coaching to combat incompetence.

Keeping no record of wrongs doesn't mean a leader has permission to sanction incompetence.

Is This a Communication Issue?

Some of the biggest mistakes I've made have been in the area of miscommunication.

Leaders can't hold people accountable for unrealistic, unspoken expectations. Expectations must be clear and concise, and they must be communicated often in order for people to internalize them.

If someone on the team does something wrong, good leaders always question themselves before they begin questioning the other person.

Recently I was giving a presentation in front of a large group of people and was using a Scripture verse to make my point. When it came time for me to put up the slide with the Scripture, I immediately noticed that it was the wrong passage.

My first instinct was anger; after all, I'd sent my notes to the people putting together the presentation. How could they screw this up?

Before I opened my mouth, though, it occurred to me that it would be wise to look at the notes I'd sent.

I was glad I did, because as it turned out, I'd sent them the wrong passage. It wasn't their fault—it was my own miscommunication.

Is This a Character Issue?

Consistency, competence, and communication all pale in comparison to the issue of character.

When we lead someone who consistently shows weak moral character, we must face it head-on. If we refuse to deal with things like dishonesty, a lack of integrity, or immorality, we are showing irresponsible leadership.

Talking with the person about a perceived lack of character is not keeping track of wrongs; it's a proactive step to make sure these issues don't build up into a bigger problem in the future. Sometimes leaders won't deal with a character issue because the person is "producing" or is perceived to be irreplaceable. However, if we refuse to deal with these issues, they always come back to bite the organization. When people see team members get away with actions that don't fit the vision of the organization, it sends a message about what the company or team truly values. A true leader knows what they stand for, and they uphold those standards with their team as well.

* * *

The difference between effective leaders and ineffective leaders isn't that effective leaders never have to deal with people's mistakes. Instead, they know how to get to the roots of problems when they come up so they can solve them in a way that builds up the individual and the rest of the organization.

Excellent leaders don't use someone's past to attack their future. Instead of keeping a record of wrongs, they forgive and then find a constructive way forward.

QUESTIONS TO HELP YOU LEAD IN THE MOST EXCELLENT WAY

Questions to Ask Yourself

1. What wrongs are in my record book that I need to deal with?
2. Is there anything I'm holding over someone's head that I haven't spoken with them about yet?

Questions to Ask Your Team

1. Is there anything you've wanted to say to me for a long time but haven't had the opportunity to do so?
2. Is there anything we're holding back from doing because of past failures?

SUMMARY STATEMENTS

→ The tone the leader sets eventually becomes the tone of the entire organization.

→ It's possible to become so obsessed with what people are doing wrong that we lose sight of all they're doing right.

→ If a problem is consistent, it demands a conversation.

→ Leaders can't hold people accountable for unrealistic, unspoken expectations.

#BestWayToLead

CHAPTER 11

DOES NOT DELIGHT IN EVIL

Love does not delight in evil.
1 CORINTHIANS 13:6

HAVE YOU EVER ENJOYED SOMETHING that wasn't good for you?

Earlier in this book I mentioned my absolute love for desserts. One of my top-five favorite desserts on the planet is something called a Baked Apple Dumplin from Cracker Barrel.

I honestly don't have words to describe how amazing this dessert is. It's essentially a huge dumpling covered with cooked apples, cinnamon, cinnamon-flavored breadcrumbs, and about a gallon of vanilla ice cream.

For years I enjoyed this dessert, and I couldn't pass up ordering it whenever I ate at Cracker Barrel.

Until recently.

I was browsing a magazine and (unfortunately) discovered that a Baked Apple Dumplin has approximately 3,229 calories.

Dang!

That's more calories than my body needs for an entire *day*.

How is it possible to enjoy something so much when it's horrible for me?

As leaders, we're constantly presented with the temptation to embrace things that will harm us. And one of these things that goes down just as sweetly as a Baked Apple Dumplin is the temptation to delight in evil.

The next item in the apostle Paul's description of leadership is that "love does not delight in evil" (1 Corinthians 13:6).

We don't usually go out seeking evil; the problem is that we often don't recognize evil for what it is. We are completely unaware about its true nature—the way I used to be about the Baked Apple Dumplin.

Most of us would take a look at the phrase "delight in evil" and automatically assume it refers to some sort of sexual scandal, or perhaps a financial downfall. Most of us would look at such major evils and then move on, certain we don't fall into this category.

But what if evil sometimes comes packaged as something normal or harmless—just a part of life as we know it?

WARNING SIGNS YOU'RE DELIGHTING IN EVIL

Since the world's definition of evil is different from God's perspective, we need to be intentional about recognizing it so we can guard against it in our lives and leadership. Here are three indicators to help us determine if we are delighting in evil.

Do You Delight in Being Right All the Time?

Do you constantly imagine yourself in an argument with someone (perhaps a coworker, a boss, a parent, or a spouse), and in the argument you are "telling them like it is"—verbally ripping them to shreds? Maybe there's even a crowd gathered around, and just like in middle school, they all say, "Ooh" whenever you make a point that takes a serious bite out of your opponent.

I'm guessing we've all had a fantasy like this at some point or another. However, if we find ourselves constantly obsessing over being right, we're delighting in evil. Even if this tearing down of other people happens only in our heads, it still undermines our effectiveness as leaders, because the way we think about others eventually affects the way we lead them.

The apostle Paul gives some incredible leadership advice in 2 Corinthians 10:5: "We capture their rebellious thoughts and teach them to obey Christ" (NLT). When we take hold of our negative thoughts and refuse to allow them to dominate our attitudes toward other people, we are able to lead more effectively.

The way we think about other people is the launching pad for how we lead with our actions.

Do You Delight in Seeing Other People Fail?

Do you enjoy seeing other people (especially people in your industry) fail? Anytime we privately celebrate the pain and suffering of another person (even if they work for an opposing company or church or team), we are delighting in evil. Think about it: how twisted is it to celebrate when someone makes a mistake, commits a sin, or falls from a prominent place of prestige? This is an indication that something is broken inside us.

Let's go back to the story of David for a moment.

This guy tasted success when he defeated Goliath, but then Saul made his life a living nightmare.

Saul lied about David.

Saul made false assumptions about David.

Saul made it impossible for David to live in peace.

Saul forced David to run for his life.

If I'm David, the one thing I want is for something bad to happen to Saul.

The last chapter of 1 Samuel tells the story of how Saul's life came to an end. It's one of the most tragic scenes in Scripture as we see a man who once had so much potential die in battle, and his sons with him.

You'd think this would be the most joyous news in the world to David; after all, now he could live in peace and maybe even step into the role of leadership the Lord had promised him years before.

The Bible gives us a peek into what happened when David found out about Saul's death:

> David and his men tore their clothes in sorrow when they
> heard the news. They mourned and wept and fasted all
> day for Saul and his son Jonathan, and for the LORD's
> army and the nation of Israel, because they had died by
> the sword that day.
> 2 SAMUEL 1:11-12, NLT

David didn't throw a "Saul is dead" party; he didn't celebrate the demise of his enemy; he didn't sit around gloating with his friends. Instead, he was broken over the fall of Saul, his enemy.

I have to wonder, *How in the world do I become a person like that?*

It's a question we all need to address as leaders: How do we become people who love and care about those who have zero love and affection for us?

The truth is that 99.9 percent of leaders are highly competitive (the other .1 percent are liars). And if we aren't careful, we'll begin to look at everyone else in our line of work or ministry as people we need to tear down rather than build up.

David's reaction of genuine grief over Saul's death had a profound impact on the people who surrounded him. His reaction became their reaction. I believe it also caused his team to buy in to his leadership a little bit more, because they could see the evidence that David really did care about others.

You can tell a person's true character by how they speak about those who have fallen.

Do You Delight in Pointing Out Others' Failures?

Do you like to be the person to inform others about someone's failures? If our go-to reaction when we hear about a sin or shortcoming is to be the first to share the news with as many people as possible, then we're delighting in evil. This is especially true when we know only half of the story and fill in the missing parts with what we believe is the truth.

Social media may make it easier to share news with a big audience, but the problem of broadcasting other people's failure is not a new thing. When Saul died, there was a guy who wanted to make sure he was the one to tell David. In fact, it could be argued from the text that he embellished the story a little to make himself look good.

After the death of Saul, David returned from his victory over the Amalekites and spent two days in Ziklag. On the third day a man arrived from Saul's army camp. He had torn his clothes and put dirt on his head to show that he was in mourning. He fell to the ground before David in deep respect.

"Where have you come from?" David asked.

"I escaped from the Israelite camp," the man replied.

"What happened?" David demanded. "Tell me how the battle went."

The man replied, "Our entire army fled from the battle. Many of the men are dead, and Saul and his son Jonathan are also dead."

"How do you know Saul and Jonathan are dead?" David demanded of the young man.

The man answered, "I happened to be on Mount Gilboa, and there was Saul leaning on his spear with the enemy chariots and charioteers closing in on him. When he turned and saw me, he cried out for me to come to him. 'How can I help?' I asked him.

"He responded, 'Who are you?'

"'I am an Amalekite,' I told him.

"Then he begged me, 'Come over here and put me out of my misery, for I am in terrible pain and want to die.'

"So I killed him," the Amalekite told David, "for I knew he couldn't live. Then I took his crown and his armband, and I have brought them here to you, my lord."

2 SAMUEL 1:1-10, NLT

No doubt this dude thought he was about to be rewarded for sharing the news of Saul's death with David. Maybe he thought he'd be given money or a leadership position—or both. In any case, there was a passion driving him to deliver the bad news.

However, things didn't turn out so well for him:

David said to the young man who had brought the news, "Where are you from?"

And he replied, "I am a foreigner, an Amalekite, who lives in your land."

"Why were you not afraid to kill the LORD's anointed one?" David asked.

Then David said to one of his men, "Kill him!" So the man thrust his sword into the Amalekite and killed him. "You have condemned yourself," David said, "for you yourself confessed that you killed the LORD's anointed one."

2 SAMUEL 1:13-16, NLT

If this guy made up the story about killing Saul, it didn't serve him well.

If he did kill Saul and then succumbed to his desire to boast, that didn't serve him well either.

The way we talk about the faults and failures of others screams volumes about us to the people we lead. If they see us as having to be the "informant," pointing out where someone has fallen short, then their trust level will begin to decline. They will eventually come to the conclusion that when they make a mistake themselves, we'll be talking *about* them rather than *to* them.

One more thing about this before we move on: the reason most leaders like to be the bearers of bad news is because we struggle with our own insecurities. We have the idea that as long as we can point to what others are doing wrong, we don't have to look in the mirror and deal with the issues that are right in front of us.

To be effective leaders, we need to be secure enough in who we are and in what God has called us to do that we build our teams up instead of tearing them down.

STEPS TO AVOID DELIGHTING IN EVIL

In my experience, I've found that it's easy to fall into delighting in evil without even realizing it. With that in mind, here are four commitments I've made that have helped me fight this tendency in my own leadership.

Publicly and Intentionally Celebrate the Success of Others

Whenever I see someone move the ball a little bit further down the field, I want to be the guy who celebrates progress, not the one who criticizes the play. If another church or ministry is focused on Christ and reaching people, then it's not my place to criticize how they do things or whether I like their music style; I want to champion them as much as I champion the church I'm a part of.

Refuse to Be the "Let Me Tell You What's Really Going On" Person

Maybe you've been in this conversation before (I know I have): someone is talking up all the good things another business or church has accomplished, until one of the listeners can't stand it any longer. They say something like, "Yeah, all that is great, but if you knew some of the things I know, you wouldn't be saying all that good stuff."

This response is almost always based in jealousy and insecurity, neither of which is a solid foundation for building excellent leadership.

There are times when certain information should be communicated; however, it's always best if that's done in a private setting so people can ask questions and get clarification, and so false assumptions don't take root.

Remember That It Could Be You

A few years ago something switched in the way I view people's sin and failures.

A pastor I knew was caught having an affair, and I saw how it absolutely destroyed his family and his ministry.

At first I was highly critical of this guy, and every time I spoke about the situation, the words that flowed out of me were full of anger and condemnation.

Then one night it occurred to me that if it weren't for the grace of God in my own life, I could do exactly what the other guy did.

It's easy to be condemning of others when we haven't walked their circumstances.

Don't get me wrong—I'm not trying to justify what this guy did. I'm just saying that when we judge other people's mistakes and believe we're somehow above them, we're setting ourselves up for colossal failure.

Being excellent leaders means we don't approach people who have messed up through the lens of condemnation; rather, we seek to hear their story and try to see them the way God sees them.

Don't Allow Negative Thoughts about Others to Dominate Your Mind

If we allow negative, critical, and disheartening thoughts to dominate our minds, we will sabotage our ability to lead effectively.

If I have a problem with someone, the best way I've found to make sure I'm not overcome with negative thoughts about them is to have a personal, one-on-one conversation with them. The goal is to have a respectful, honest conversation about the problem and then give them a chance to help me see if there's anything I'm missing or if I'm perceiving things the wrong way.

The longer we allow negativity and pessimism toward another person to dominate our thought patterns, the less effective we'll be in leading them.

The apostle Paul writes about the urgency of settling matters quickly:

"Don't sin by letting anger control you." Don't let the
sun go down while you are still angry, for anger gives
a foothold to the devil.
EPHESIANS 4:26-27, NLT

We already talked about this in chapter 7, but I think it's worth repeating: if you need to have a serious conversation with someone and it's likely emotions will run high, it needs to be done in person. E-MAIL DOESN'T WORK, TEXTING DOESN'T WORK, AND SOCIAL MEDIA DOESN'T WORK.

Sorry for the all-caps screaming, but this is something I'm passionate about. It's a lesson I learned the hard way, and I don't want you to go through the same thing.

If we're going to do an excellent job leading people, we must embrace the uncomfortable and love them enough to have a face-to-face conversation. Genuine care and concern for a person can't be communicated electronically.

TEN SIGNS OF AN INSECURE LEADER

Not delighting in evil demands that we intentionally fight insecurity. I encourage you to reflect on these ten signs of an insecure leader to see if any of them describe you.

1. You see people as working for you, not with you.
2. Everyone who pushes back on your ideas is automatically branded as disloyal. (For an insecure leader, the definition of loyalty is "You must love everything I say and do!")

3. Every time someone says something good about someone else, you feel the need to bring up "the truth" about the person, but you frame it in a way that makes you seem like you're speaking out of concern for them.

4. Jealousy is your go-to reaction when someone you lead is recognized for the incredible job they've done but you aren't mentioned.

5. You can't celebrate when another person or organization wins.

6. You are constantly plagued by the belief that someone on your team will eventually attempt a coup and seize your leadership position.

7. You dismiss something incredible that's happening in another organization or church because it doesn't exactly line up with your methodology or theology.

8. You lead through intimidation, always threatening to fire someone if things don't get better.

9. You like the fact that people on your staff are afraid of you.

10. You enjoy fighting *with* people more than fighting *for* them.

As leaders, all of us have dealt with insecurity on some level. In fact, the more our church has grown, the more I seem to catch insecurity rearing its head. Some days I feel like I'm playing "whack-a-mole" with all the insecurities that rise to the surface.

If you are dealing with one or more of these signs, stop for a second and celebrate, because the first step to solving a problem is admitting there's a problem in the first place. Then you can begin to deal rationally with the fears that plague you and build confidence based on your identity in who God has made you to be.

Security in leadership is the result of sanity in our thinking.

QUESTIONS TO HELP YOU LEAD IN THE MOST EXCELLENT WAY

Questions to Ask Yourself

1. How do I respond when I see others fail? How do I respond when I see others succeed?
2. Are there any thoughts I'm delighting in that would be embarrassing if they came to light?

Questions to Ask Your Team

1. Do you agree that insecurity can lead people to delight in evil? Why or why not?
2. What are some healthy ways we could celebrate people's successes here? What are some healthy ways we could respond when someone makes a mistake?

SUMMARY STATEMENTS

→ Anytime we privately celebrate the pain and suffering of another person, we are delighting in evil.

→ You can tell a person's true character by how they speak about those who have fallen.

→ The longer we allow negativity and pessimism to dominate our thought patterns, the less effective we'll be as leaders.

→ Genuine care and concern for a person can't be communicated electronically.

#BestWayToLead

CHAPTER 12

REJOICES WITH THE TRUTH

Love . . . rejoices with the truth.

1 CORINTHIANS 13:6

"WHAT'S THAT SPOT ON YOUR BACK?" Lucretia asked.

"I don't know—I've never seen my back," I shot back with a smile.

"No, seriously. There's a spot on your back, and it doesn't look good."

Let me pause here and say that Lucretia is a medical doctor and is incredibly sensitive to spots on people's skin. Her own father went through a battle with melanoma, so this isn't a joking matter for her.

She examined my back a little more. "I think you should get it checked out."

"Okay, sure," I agreed.

About three months later, we were getting ready for work, and I hadn't put on my shirt yet. I heard Lucretia say, "Wow!" and immediately I knew the extra weight lifting I'd been doing at the gym had paid off. She was in awe of the way my body was taking shape!

This was *not* the case.

"Perry, that spot on your back is getting bigger," she said. "It really doesn't look good. Did you ever schedule an appointment to get it checked out?"

Silence.

"Perry, this is a big deal. You really need to get someone to look at it."

"Okay, okay, I'll make the call today."

I didn't, and about four more months went by. The next time Lucretia saw the spot, let me just say there was a tad bit of tension in the conversation. I don't remember all the details, but I'm pretty sure I said "I'm sorry" a whole bunch.

I finally agreed to have the stupid spot looked at, knowing there were far better things I could have been doing with my time.

The doctor examined the spot and took a sample from it, and then she left to test it.

When she returned, she said, "Perry, you have skin cancer. It's pretty deep. We're going to have to schedule surgery so you can get it cut out."

All of a sudden the spot on my back was no longer a mere annoyance; it was a major deal, and it would cause my life to change pretty dramatically for the next season.

I had to cancel a vacation I'd been looking forward to.

I had to move meetings around to schedule the surgery.

And I had to go through the pain associated with the surgery.

While being patched up after the surgeon dug into my back, I said, "Hey, doc, my wife discovered the spot about a year or so ago. If I'd gotten it checked out then, do you think all this would have been necessary?"

"Oh no," he said. "If we'd gotten to this last year when it was small, we could have either treated it with some cream or done a five-minute procedure that would have had you back to normal in no time at all."

I wanted to find a time machine, travel back to when I told Lucretia it wasn't a big deal, and smack myself silly!

Lucretia had told me the truth, and I had ignored it. I thought the problem would just go away and life would go on as usual. But it didn't. Because I didn't deal with the issue, it became a much deeper problem. It ended up costing me more time, money, and pain because I'd ignored it for so long.

If I'd accepted the truth sooner, the outcome would have been a lot less painful.

One of the biggest downfalls leaders face is ignoring the truth. That's why this topic is addressed in our leadership passage: "Love . . . rejoices with the truth" (1 Corinthians 13:6).

Some of the biggest leadership mistakes came at times when I tried to either explain away—or even pray away—the truth.

As leaders, we can fall into the trap of viewing people who tell us the truth as the enemy. Instead of listening to them, we may seek to punish them. Excellent leaders, however, are willing to receive the truth, even when it's hard.

David eventually became the king of Israel. In the first several chapters of 2 Samuel, we see that he was enjoying a season of kicking butt and taking names. But then he made some really poor choices—namely, committing adultery with a woman named Bathsheba, who became pregnant with his child.

Meanwhile, Bathsheba's husband was at war, fighting for David. David had him brought home, hoping he would go "see his wife" so the child could be explained. However, Bathsheba's husband was so serious about his commitment to his military and his country that he refused to take advantage of the offer.

So David essentially had this guy murdered, married Bathsheba, and hoped things in the kingdom would go back to normal.

The last verse in this chapter simply says, "But the LORD was displeased with what David had done" (2 Samuel 11:27, NLT).

We live in a culture that has more freedom of expression than at any other time in history. We are free to disagree with spiritual leaders, local government, and even the president. We can express our outrage through marches, demonstrations, or rants on social media. We can say just about anything, about just about anyone, and receive very little pushback.

But that's not the way things were in David's day.

You did not say anything bad about the king.

And you absolutely did not say anything bad *to* the king.

Doing so could get you time in jail or even cost you your life.

So while there were plenty of people who knew what David had done, no one had the courage to speak truthfully to him for fear it would not be good for their careers—or their livelihoods.

Except for one guy—Nathan.

David had a friend, a prophet named Nathan, whom we first met in 2 Samuel 7. David's actions hadn't escaped Nathan's attention, and because Nathan cared more about doing what was right rather than what was easy, he took a risk and confronted David.

The LORD sent Nathan the prophet to tell David this story: "There were two men in a certain town. One was rich, and one was poor. The rich man owned a great many sheep and cattle. The poor man owned nothing but one little lamb he had bought. He raised that little lamb, and it grew up with his children. It ate from the man's own plate and drank from his cup. He cuddled it in his arms like a baby daughter. One day a guest arrived at the home of the rich man. But instead of killing an animal from his own flock or herd, he took the poor man's lamb and killed it and prepared it for his guest."

2 SAMUEL 12:1-4, NLT

Nathan didn't kick open the palace doors, punch the guards in the throat, and grab David around his neck. He began with a story, understanding that the approach is everything when dealing with delicate situations like this one.

Nathan's story invoked a strong response from David.

> David was furious. "As surely as the LORD lives," he
> vowed, "any man who would do such a thing deserves
> to die! He must repay four lambs to the poor man for
> the one he stole and for having no pity."
>
> 2 SAMUEL 12:5-6, NLT

I'm guessing that right about now you're shaking your head. How in the world could David have been so hypocritical? How could he not see the setup? Why could he be passionate about justice for someone else when he had committed a serious injustice himself?

It's simple: David had blind spots, just like we all do.

The other day I was backing out of a parking space when all of a sudden, I heard a guy screaming like a banshee, telling me to stop. I slammed on my brakes and stared at him like he was smoking crack. He pointed to a car that was also backing out, which I couldn't see because it was in my blind spot.

I was so thankful for this guy who was willing to risk looking like an idiot so I didn't crush the car behind me.

One of the reasons we need to rejoice in the truth, whether that means sharing it or receiving it, is because every leader has blind spots. Good leaders are willing to reach down deep, muster up their courage, and have those tough conversations.

That's what Nathan did.

Nathan said to David, "You are that man! The LORD, the God of Israel, says: I anointed you king of Israel and saved you from the power of Saul. I gave you your master's house and his wives and the kingdoms of Israel and Judah. And if that had not been enough, I would have given you much, much more. Why, then, have you despised the word of the LORD and done this horrible deed? For you have murdered Uriah the Hittite with the sword of the Ammonites and stolen his wife."

2 SAMUEL 12:7-9, NLT

Nathan didn't sugarcoat anything; he got straight to the point. Why? I believe he had this kind of courage because he valued the Lord's call on his life more than the convenience of sitting on the sidelines, keeping his mouth shut.

Nathan confronted David not because he wanted to condemn him but rather out of sincere concern for him. After all, that's what excellent leaders do.

HOW TO GIVE AND RECEIVE HARD TRUTHS

Practically speaking, how does truth telling play itself out in our lives? The following four concepts have helped me immensely when it comes to rejoicing in the truth, whether giving it or receiving it.

Stop Making Excuses

Leaders who make excuses never make a difference.

Can you imagine this story from Nathan's point of view? Up to this point, his interactions with David had been positive, and he was enjoying a position in David's inner circle. No doubt he was pretty popular in the palace.

He could have told God he didn't think it would be the best move for his career to call out the king. He could have formed a committee to study the situation to figure out the best approach. He could have said that he'd just pray about it and hope everything would eventually work out.

Leaders are often guilty of making excuses like this. If we're in a business environment, we may use marketplace conditions, the economy, or the government to justify being passive and not doing the hard thing. If we're leaders in a ministry or church, we may use prayer as an excuse not to step up and deal with the issue the Lord has called us to lead our people through.

But Nathan chose conviction over convenience, putting his career and personal comfort on the line in order to tell some hard news. He approached David in grace and truth and dealt with the issue everyone else seemed to be avoiding.

What was the result? David admitted he'd messed up and got back on track as a leader. If Nathan hadn't cared about him enough to have the uncomfortable conversation with him, there's no telling how unfocused and even destructive David could have become in his leadership.

I wish this were easy, but it's not.

In a church I formerly served in, there was a popular Bible study among the young married people in our church. At least twenty couples attended, and the hallways were always buzzing after the class was dismissed.

Then the leader of the class took some time away from teaching, and a new guy was put in charge of the class. It went from twenty couples to four couples in just four weeks.

It was obvious that the new guy couldn't teach, had zero people skills, and was boring people to the point that they were consider-ing diving out the window!

I had a conversation with the pastor I was serving with and watched him wrestle with doing the right thing. On one hand, he didn't want to hurt the guy's feelings; after all, the pastor was the one who had placed him in this leadership position and told him he thought he would be a good fit.

But the epic drop in attendance and the feedback from the people who had bailed made it obvious that a tough decision would have to be made.

I watched as my pastor had a hard but loving conversation with this guy and moved him out of this position. It was one of the most powerful leadership lessons I've seen. A new teacher was put in place, and the class exploded in size just like before.

At first the guy who had been "demoted" took it pretty hard; however, my pastor eventually found a new place for him to vol-unteer, and he wound up thriving rather than just surviving from week to week.

My pastor could have blamed the people in the class, saying they just didn't appreciate "deep teaching" and making them feel spiritually inferior. But instead of denying reality, he made a tough call for the good of the entire group.

If you're facing an issue with the people you lead, you must step into the uncomfortable. Your call is the one all excellent leaders face: to approach the situation with compassion but be willing to speak the truth, no matter the cost.

Weigh People's Opinions; Don't Count Them

Not long ago, I was battling a season of intense scrutiny on social media. It seemed like everyone with a smartphone and an opinion about me felt the obligation to share it with the world. Even though I knew I shouldn't pay attention to this feedback or allow it to bother me, it began to weigh on me more heavily than just about anything I'd dealt with before.

I spoke to a friend of mine who is about twenty years older than I am and way smarter, and he told me, "Opinions should be weighed, not counted."

I didn't understand what he was saying at first, but as he explained it to me, this truth began to set me free.

Everyone in this world has an opinion about everything, and social media has made it easy and convenient to share those opinions. His counsel to me was that there will always be people who don't like me or what I'm doing, but when it comes to listening to people, everyone's opinion shouldn't carry equal weight.

For example, let's say you have to make an unpopular but necessary decision in your organization. As a result, a lot of people become mad at you, and they begin to question your motives and intelligence and even jump to unfair conclusions about your character.

They say things like, "Well, if I were the leader, I would [fill in the blank]" or "It would have been a better idea to do such-and-such." They aren't short on their opinions, even if they've never been a leader in this context before.

It's easy to criticize a sermon when you've never preached one.

It's easy to criticize a musical performance when you've never played an instrument.

It's easy to criticize a football player when you've never strapped on a helmet.

Which is why, when it comes to who we listen to, opinions should be weighed, not counted.

I'm going to take a guess here and say that if a random person had walked in from off the street and started launching verbal grenades at David, that guy probably would have been taking a dirt nap by the end of the day.

However, Nathan was someone David knew, respected, and trusted. Because of Nathan's proximity to the king, David was receptive to what Nathan had to say, even though it wasn't what he wanted to hear.

This is why it's essential to be surrounded by a team of people who know you—really know you—beyond just who you are at the office or at church or in class.

I've heard leaders say, "It's lonely at the top." But I think that's true only when leaders choose to isolate themselves and not bring anyone to the top with them.

There's no greater asset for leaders than a group of people who will surround them, care about them, and refuse to let them make self-centered decisions. These "Nathans" can see the damage these choices would cause to leaders and to the organizations they lead.

I'm grateful I made the decision a while ago to surround myself with people who love Jesus, love NewSpring, and love me (in that order). We are a team that not only knows each other in an office setting but also enjoys doing life together as much as possible.

This type of leadership circle has made it safe for me to have hard conversations with my teammates, and it's made it easier for them to talk with me as well. We value the person more than the position, and that creates an environment where the truth can be given and received.

Don't Ignore the Obvious Truths

When I surrendered my life to Christ at eighteen years old, I did so in a great church.

One of the things that stands out to me about the church was how incredible the music was. Every time someone got up to sing, the music was guaranteed to be awesome, and whenever the choir sang a song, they absolutely nailed it.

I had a little bit of singing ability in me, so I asked the music director about the possibility of my singing one Sunday. He told me I would need to come to an audition—which was pretty much the end of my singing career.

The concept was simple: if a person couldn't sing, they simply weren't allowed to belt out a solo in front of the congregation. The leaders in the church loved people enough to tell them the truth (rather than telling them they're amazing and then watching them embarrass themselves on *American Idol* auditions).

I was inexperienced in church work and leadership at the time, so I assumed that standard of honesty was par for the course in other churches too.

I was wrong.

In my job as a part-time youth pastor at the church that was a little larger than a Mormon family, I remember waking up around 5:00 a.m. the Sunday I was going to be introduced to the church. I was so excited about my new leadership role that I could hardly wait to get up and get dressed.

On that particular Sunday, right before the message, "special music" was slated for the service. I was pretty pumped because I love music and, based on my experiences at my previous church, I knew I was in for a treat.

A gentleman we will refer to as Kyle nervously walked to the platform and picked up the microphone. When the taped music began to play behind him, he gave it all he had.

The only word I can think of to describe what I felt in that moment is *terror*.

I don't have words to explain how awful his singing was. Honestly, I think listening to cows die in a hailstorm would have been more bearable. It took me less than ten seconds to grasp the reality that Kyle didn't have a single ounce of musical talent in his body.

After the song was over, a few people said, "Amen." I may have muttered, "Thank You, God"—not because the music was good, but rather because it was over. Kyle walked back to where his family was seated, and the service went on.

The very next week, Kyle sang the special music again.

He hadn't improved at all from the week before, and I pretended I had to go to the restroom so my ears wouldn't have to experience what I will refer to as "waterboarding for the ears."

The following Monday I was at the church office, still getting acquainted with my new role, when one of the people who hired me stopped by to see how I was doing.

We made small talk for a few minutes, and then, even though I knew this might cause some issues, I had to ask about Kyle and why he was allowed near the platform. Who in the world thought it was a good idea to give him a microphone?

My colleague explained to me that no one in the church enjoyed Kyle's singing; in fact, they all pretty much shared my opinion. However, because they didn't want to hurt Kyle's feelings, they just let him keep singing.

"Kyle really does have a good heart," he said.

My response was, "Maybe so, but his voice is horrible! And unfortunately, when he sings, I'm not hearing his heart; I'm hearing his voice."

This went on for several months until the church hired a new pastor. I was relieved because I knew the second he heard one of Kyle's songs, he would do something about it.

I will never forget the look on the pastor's face the first time he heard Kyle sing. He looked confused as the song began, obviously wondering what was happening. Then a look of pain swept across his face as he tried to smile but only managed to look constipated. Finally he bowed his head, as if he were praying. But I knew that trick—he was desperately asking Jesus to come back immediately so he wouldn't have to endure this any longer.

The following Monday I walked into the pastor's office, and after a few minutes, the subject of Kyle came up.

"Pastor, what did you think of the special music?" I asked.

He laughed and shook his head but wouldn't say anything.

I pressed him for an answer. "Are you going to make sure Kyle doesn't 'bless us' with his singing anymore?"

"No, I'm just going to let it be."

I encouraged him to deal with this reality, but he wouldn't budge.

"I don't want to hurt Kyle's feelings."

What about the fact that Kyle is hurting the feelings of everyone in the church? I thought.

I served at that church just over two years, and Kyle continued to sing regularly.

As I look back on that situation, it makes me sad. Everyone in the church knew Kyle couldn't sing. On the Sundays when we had visitors show up and Kyle was singing, I wanted to sit by them and apologize profusely as he wailed. No one loved Kyle enough to tell him the truth, and everyone suffered as a result.

At this point you may think I'm being a little too tough on Kyle. (I would argue that you didn't have to listen to what I had to listen to.) Kyle was a great guy. He worked hard. He brought his family to church. He was willing to do just about anything to serve. However, he couldn't sing, and allowing him to do so was not an act of love but an act of cowardice.

As leaders, we are guaranteed to face situations when someone we lead isn't able to do their job well or is going down a destructive path. If we refuse to say anything because we're afraid we might upset them, we're not loving them well.

In most cases when someone isn't excelling in their job, they know it, and they're feeling unbelievable amounts of stress in their lives. If you swallow hard and have a difficult conversation, the person may respond not with anger but with relief. They knew they weren't the best at what they were doing, but they didn't want to quit or ask for help because they were afraid of appearing weak.

I tell people I serve with on the leadership team, "Please don't ever allow me to become the emperor with no clothes." I don't want to be the guy everyone sits around and tells, "Yes, sir, boss, anything you say, boss. You really killed that sermon, boss" while keeping their real opinions to themselves.

If I'm going to be an excellent leader, I need those closest to me to speak truthfully at all times, even when it's uncomfortable.

Let me push the pause button here and say that an invitation to speak the truth doesn't give people permission to be complete rear ends and always come up with a "truth" to share just for the sake of arguing. That's a sign of insecurity, not good leadership.

Several years ago, we had a young man on our staff who pushed back on every idea other people shared.

After watching this behavior in several meetings, I decided to ask him about it in private. His attitude was causing the rest of the staff to leave him out of discussions because they didn't want to deal with a "negative Nancy"!

He told me that he thought the ideas other people shared were often excellent. However, he followed that up by saying, "It's just that I've always felt the need to play devil's advocate in the meetings I attend."

I calmly (but directly) informed him that the devil didn't really need an advocate.

I also explained to him that we worked in a church, which meant we weren't necessarily supposed to be representing the devil.

It was a tough conversation, but eventually he admitted that being an antagonist wasn't an indication of excellent leadership but rather a sign of insecurity.

Wise leaders are able to step in and address problems directly—without resorting to antagonism.

Admit Your Mistakes

The most dangerous leaders on the planet are the ones who refuse to admit their mistakes.

David was busted. There was no way he could escape Nathan's confrontation of his sin. He could have had Nathan killed or imprisoned, but it wouldn't have changed the fact he'd messed up and his issues were now exposed.

That's when David uttered one of the most humble sentences a leader has ever said:

> David confessed to Nathan, "I have sinned against the LORD."
>
> 2 SAMUEL 12:13, NLT

David didn't try to conceal the fact he'd messed up; he confessed his sin openly.

One of the reservations leaders have about admitting they've messed up is the fear of letting people see their weaknesses and faults. All too often, we believe we have to have everything together, with no faults or flaws. We assume that admitting we made a mistake just isn't an option.

That was not the case with David. In fact, it didn't take him hours to process what Nathan had confronted him with. He confessed quickly and publicly.

Can you imagine what David's confession did for those who followed him? I would argue that it caused them to see him as strong, not weak. I believe it relieved pressure on them and allowed them to conclude, "Well, his life isn't perfect, so I don't have to pretend mine is either." This must have resulted in an incredible amount of buy-in from his team because they knew their leader would be honest, even when the consequences impacted him personally.

I met Christ in 1990; however, I struggled with an addiction to pornography until 1999. Finally, through confessing my addiction to a friend and establishing some strong lines of accountability—and with a lot of help from God—I was able to overcome my addiction.

In 2002, I was preaching on the subject of pornography and its dangers, and toward the end of the message, I felt like I should tell the church how I'd personally struggled and overcome.

Fear flooded my mind. *There's no way I can tell them that,* I thought. *People will use it to attack me and tear me down.*

I had an internal battle for a while, and in the end I wound up saying that I knew victory over pornography was possible because I had struggled with it myself and had been given the strength to stay away from it.

So many men responded to the invitation for prayer that particular Sunday that we had to seize every staff member present to accommodate the flood of people.

When I asked men why they responded, the number one

answer was, "When you said you had struggled with this, I knew it was okay to say I was struggling as well."

It wasn't my strength that served as an inspiration to the men that day; it was my weakness. God used my admission of failure and my honesty about the battle I'd fought to bring people to confession.

All leaders will mess up at some point; the question is whether they will have the character to admit they messed up and ask for help.

Nathan confronted David, and David was better for it. He was a leader who really could rejoice in the truth, even when it hurt.

In a culture where political correctness is the highest value, we desperately need excellent leaders who are committed to building a culture of radical honesty.

QUESTIONS TO HELP YOU LEAD IN THE MOST EXCELLENT WAY

Questions to Ask Yourself

1. Is there anyone I'm afraid to have a hard conversation with because it might hurt their feelings?
2. Am I holding anyone back because I'm afraid to tell them the truth?
3. How can I celebrate and reward honesty this week?

Questions to Ask Your Team

1. On a scale of 1 to 10 (with 1 being not a priority at all and 10 being the highest priority), how much is honesty valued in our organization?
2. What would it take for us to get to a 10?

3. On a scale of 1 to 10, how comfortable do you feel being honest with me?

4. What's one thing we've been trying to deny as a team that we need to roll up our sleeves and deal with?

5. What's one truth about me that you're afraid to tell me?

SUMMARY STATEMENTS

→ Excellent leaders are willing to receive the truth, even when it's hard.

→ Good leaders are willing to reach down deep, muster up their courage, and have those tough conversations.

→ We should value the Lord's call on our lives more than the convenience of sitting on the sidelines.

→ Leaders should approach a situation with compassion but be willing to speak the truth, no matter the cost.

→ The most dangerous leaders on the planet are the ones who refuse to admit their mistakes.

#BestWayToLead

CHAPTER 13

ALWAYS PROTECTS

Love . . . always protects.
1 CORINTHIANS 13:6-7

I HAD TO GO TO COURT ONCE.

I'd gotten a speeding ticket, and I decided to try to contest it. I heard that the judge who presided over the cases was pretty lenient toward people who showed humility. My plan was to admit to the judge that I'd been speeding and then ask him to be merciful, as I was so broke I had to go to Kentucky Fried Chicken to lick other people's fingers.

Before the traffic section of court began, I watched people who had been arrested the previous night appear before the judge for sentencing.

One dude who stood before the judge was so redneck he made the cast of *Duck Dynasty* look like royalty.

The arresting officer explained the reason for the arrest, describing the domestic disturbance this guy had caused and mentioning that he'd used offensive language in front of a six-year-old boy who was at the scene.

After the officer was finished, Captain Redneck said, "Your honor, can I say something?"

"Sure," the judge replied.

"I just want you to know that six-year-old kid cusses more than me."

Everyone in the courtroom lost it. I had to laugh to keep from crying. Here was a dude who had obviously partaken in a beer or twelve the night before and gotten himself into a world of trouble. However, instead of accepting the blame, he thought the best course of action was to throw the "cussing kid" under the bus, somehow thinking that was going to help him.

I've never forgotten that incident and what it taught me about leadership. It served as a reminder that, if I'm going to be an excellent leader whom people want to follow, I must be willing to protect the people who work with me rather than use them as scapegoats.

People love working for leaders who fight for them rather than with them—leaders who coach them through tough situations rather than criticizing them for their mistakes.

Paul's description of an excellent leader includes these words: "Love . . . always protects" (1 Corinthians 13:6-7).

Once again, we return to the story of David.

Not only did David set an incredible example for how to lead effectively, but he also wrote about topics that are relevant for leaders. Out of the seventy-four psalms that list him as the author, the most famous is Psalm 23:

The LORD is my shepherd, I lack nothing.
     He makes me lie down in green pastures,
he leads me beside quiet waters,
     he refreshes my soul.
He guides me along the right paths
     for his name's sake.

Even though I walk
    through the darkest valley,
I will fear no evil,
    for you are with me;
your rod and your staff,
    they comfort me.

You prepare a table before me
    in the presence of my enemies.
You anoint my head with oil;
    my cup overflows.
Surely your goodness and love will follow me
    all the days of my life,
and I will dwell in the house of the LORD
    forever.

PSALM 23:1-6

If you're a leader in any context, whether it's in a corporation, a church, a small business, or a family, I believe the leadership wisdom David shares in Psalm 23 has the potential to change our perspectives as leaders, as well as the environments we lead in.

In this psalm, David describes the way God leads: He always protects, even when it doesn't appear that way.

I believe we can benefit from six ideas David communicates about the protective nature of leadership.

EXCELLENT LEADERS PROVIDE

The LORD is my shepherd, I lack nothing.

PSALM 23:1

David's insights about the Lord's character in the first five words of this psalm are powerful. He doesn't refer to the Lord as "my commander" or "my king" or "my homeboy"; rather, he calls Him his shepherd. One of the things I've learned from visiting Israel is that in Middle Eastern culture, the relationship between a shepherd and the sheep is pretty special. Sheep are unable to find food and water on their own or take care of their own medical needs, so without a shepherd to provide for them, their lifespans would be incredibly brief!

When the people we lead see us as domineering control freaks who care more about the bottom line than the people we work with, it prevents us from building a strong team or accomplishing our visions. In contrast, when people understand that we are for them, not against them, and that we want what's best for them (just like shepherds want for their sheep), they will follow us to the ends of the earth.

One thing that brings me peace in the middle of my personal leadership storms is the understanding that just as the Lord was David's shepherd, He is mine as well. If He called me to it, He will see me through it. That's not always the way I feel; however, the facts in Scripture are way beyond my feelings—and when I press into what God's Word says, I'm brought back to an understanding that God is actually for me.

Notice what David says next: "I lack nothing." Another version puts it this way: "I have all that I need" (NLT).

I'm a firm believer that leaders who are committed to following the Lord will always have all they need. Church leaders often complain to me about their lack of resources, but we have more resources, more information, and greater opportunities to spread the gospel now than at any other time in history.

All too often it's not that we don't possess what we need but that we are so busy looking around at other people and wishing we had what they have. But if we focus on all we've been given instead of what we lack, we'll be able to operate at a greater capacity.

It's important to point out here that this psalm was written more than twenty-five hundred years ago, yet the truths are still relevant to our world today. In every generation, situation, and economic condition, the Lord always provides what is needed, when it is needed.

One of the key responsibilities of leaders is to make sure the people they're leading have all they need. (Please understand: I didn't say they should have all they want! One of the biggest battles a leader must engage in is recognizing the difference between wants and needs.)

One of our main responsibilities as leaders is to make sure the people who serve with us have adequate time and resources to do the jobs required of them.

I want the people who work in the video area at NewSpring to have adequate equipment, and while they may not have what they want, they have what they need.

I want the people who work with people to have proper training to care for those who walk through the doors of our church.

I want the musicians to have the sound systems they need to be able to lead our church during worship time.

It's not their responsibility to go out and get the equipment or secure the funding for these resources. I'm the leader, and it's my job to provide what they need. It's both unwise and cruel to place demands on people without giving them the resources to deliver on what's expected of them.

Let me say this about my personal walk with the Lord and my journey as the leader of NewSpring Church: He has been faithful to provide exactly what we need, when we need it. There have been times when we've wanted something more, but He has always given us everything we need.

I would encourage you not to allow yourself to fall into the comparison trap and wish you had things the Lord has given someone else. You are called to be an excellent steward of what He has placed in your hands, and if you need something, trust that the Lord is your Shepherd. He will take care of you in ways beyond what you could imagine.

EXCELLENT LEADERS CREATE HEALTHY ENVIRONMENTS

I am very much a creature of habit.

I eat at only a handful of restaurants, and every time I go, I order pretty much the same thing.

I also love my daily routine.

I get up around five o'clock, drink a huge cup of coffee, read my Bible, get in a good workout, and then head off to the church by eight thirty or so.

I have three set meetings per week, and the rest of my time is consumed by other things that may require smaller meetings, phone calls, sermon preparation, and putting out fires.

I've heard people refer to me as "highly disciplined," since I'm pretty dedicated to my routine; however, I've been discovering lately that being committed to doing leadership one certain way all the time can actually lead to destruction over the long haul. As leaders, we sometimes need to shake things up to bring about change.

Years ago, a good friend of mine shared with me the following formula: change of place + change of pace = change of perspective.

When I first heard him say this, I thought he was one of those "artsy" guys who could never really stick to a routine.

However, as I'm continuing on my leadership journey, I am coming to understand that his formula is something we should all live and lead by if we want to help other people achieve their maximum potential.

David knew how important environments are in leadership. As a shepherd, he knew the importance of getting the sheep to the right place at the right time so they could be nourished and grow.

He talks about how the Lord did this for him: "He makes me lie down in green pastures, he leads me beside quiet waters" (Psalm 23:2).

Notice that David says the Lord "makes me lie down." God doesn't casually bring up this idea in conversation or offer it as a mere suggestion; He takes responsibility for the environment of His "sheep." His goal is to make sure we're in the best environment possible so we can receive what we need.

The environments we work and serve in really do matter. One of the ways we can protect the people we serve with from flaming out is to make sure the environment they step into every day is as safe and engaging as possible.

It's the leaders' responsibility to be sensitive to when their people are getting tired or worn out. Everyone on the planet is entitled to a bad day every once in a while; however, when a bad day turns into a negative lifestyle, leaders must care enough about the people they lead to have a conversation with the person to try to understand the problem. Is the environment invigorating them or sucking the life out of them?

Maybe the person needs a day off.

Maybe they need to take a vacation.

Maybe they need to change offices or get better lighting or have more privacy.

Maybe they need a new computer because the one they're using was bought when RadioShack was a big deal.

Maybe they just need a note of encouragement.

When you can sense that something needs to change and you step in assuming the best about a person, their buy-in to your leadership will increase exponentially.

Another thing before we move on.

One of the best things leaders can do is change their own environment (and the environment of the team) every once in a while.

Recently I felt like I'd hit a leadership wall, and I found myself sitting in my office staring at my computer screen for about fifteen minutes. Then it hit me: change of place + change of pace = change of perspective.

I packed up all my stuff, got in my car, and drove to a coffee shop. I had lunch and cleared my head, and I was able to get more done in the next four hours than I would have gotten done in four days back at my office. The "green pastures and still waters" of an unfamiliar place set my heart and mind on fire with ideas I honestly believe I wouldn't have dreamed of had I stayed in my office.

Some of the best ideas our church has ever come up with have been during staff retreats, when we get away to dream, learn, and develop ideas to take our organization to the next level. You'll never have time for these things; you have to make time. When you do, you're communicating to your people that you really care not just about the work they do but about who they are as people.

EXCELLENT LEADERS GIVE GUIDANCE

One of the worst mistakes I made as a young leader was that I wasn't willing to provide my people with enough guidance.

Several years ago, I recruited someone to help me with a major project I was working on. I let this guy know I believed in him and

I felt he could do the job really well. After a lot of persuading on my part, I finally convinced him (or maybe it was a guilt trip—I'm still not sure) to do the job.

From that point forward, we never talked about the assignment I'd given him. I didn't mentor him or explain what he was supposed to do. Come to think of it, I didn't even put any clear expectations in front of him.

He struggled for several months and then told me that this role wasn't right for him. I was young, arrogant, and clueless. I told him I thought he was a bit lazy and needed to dedicate himself more. My little pep talk didn't seem to be motivating him, however. The more I talked, the more I could see he was determined to quit.

It took me several years to realize that he gave up not because he was a bad person but rather because I'd been a bad leader. I just assumed people would know what I wanted and would do what I'd do.

Leaders can't hold people accountable for unspoken, unrealistic expectations and then go off on them because they aren't getting things done. The more time we invest in people and the more guidance we provide, the more we set them up for success.

This brings us to the next verse in Psalm 23: "He refreshes my soul. He guides me along the right paths for his name's sake" (verse 3).

God, the ultimate Leader, refreshes our souls by providing clear direction for us. We don't have to sit around and worry about the decisions before us, because in His time, He will make His direction clear.

God's guidance serves as a model for us. People with clear direction and refreshed souls will move the vision of an organization forward more effectively than any fear tactic or promise of a bonus or promotion will.

We will be much more effective when we gently guide people instead of making them feel guilty about the ways they didn't measure up.

If we really love people, we won't let them get it wrong for very long.

EXCELLENT LEADERS ARE PRESENT

At times in my leadership, I feel as if I've hit a wall. Other times I feel like I just can't do it anymore, and the world and the church would be a better place if I quit. During those seasons, I neglect to realize that the Lord is with me and wants even greater things for me than I can dream of for myself.

In the midst of those discouraging seasons, the Lord always reminds me that He is with me and that I haven't been called to do this alone. He hasn't brought me this far only for me to fail now.

One of the most important things we can do as leaders, whether we're in a family, a church or ministry setting, or a business environment, is to pray for an increasing awareness of God's presence. When we see how great the Lord is, we'll be compelled to attempt great things.

I love the honesty we see in the next verse of Psalm 23:

Even though I walk
   through the darkest valley,
I will fear no evil,
   for you are with me;
your rod and your staff,
   they comfort me.

PSALM 23:4

David didn't say he never experienced dark days but rather that in those times, he became more aware of God's presence, which gave him the strength to make it through.

How does this apply to leadership in our world?

It's simple: leaders who always protect make themselves more visible in tough times.

One of the best things an organization can do when going through a tough time is to have a leader who is calm and visibly present.

People want to know that there's a plan in place and that the right people are working on it.

I say this because many times leaders have a tendency to run, hide, or even flat-out quit when things get tough.

If you want to be an excellent leader, you have to be willing to fight through your own insecurities and make yourself visible in order to provide certainty to your people. This is precisely when they need to know that you're still in the game.

EXCELLENT LEADERS FOCUS ON BLESSINGS

As we've already established, every leader in every circle experiences criticism. At times these critics seem like mosquitoes—they're not really hurting you, but they are annoying and never seem to go away. At other times, you feel more like you've been thrown to the lions.

If you work in an environment with other believers, the criticism seems to sting even more because the Christian community seems to attach Bible verses to the bullets they fire.

It's obvious from Psalm 23 that David knew what it was like to deal with his own critics.

You prepare a table before me
    in the presence of my enemies.
You anoint my head with oil;
    my cup overflows.

PSALM 23:5

Can you imagine a table prepared by God?

I'm certain the tablecloth would be the whitest white you've ever seen.

I'm sure the place settings would put Martha Stewart to shame.

I have no doubt there would be barbecued ribs, mac and cheese, and banana pudding (all with zero calories!).

It would be the most amazing table anyone has ever had the privilege of being invited to.

But there's an interesting detail about this passage. Notice that the preparation of God's table and the presence of the enemies are mentioned in the exact same verse.

As leaders, we have a choice: we can focus on the table the Lord has placed before us, with all its blessings, benefits, potential, and opportunities. Or we can focus on the enemies who never seem to be satisfied with anything we do.

So many times I've lost sight of the blessings in my life because of the beatings I felt like I was taking.

But I've learned that where we place our focus—the table or the talkers—will ultimately result in what type of leaders we will become.

If our focus is on the table, we will lead people with hope, clear vision, and a willingness to work through the tough times. If our focus is on our enemies, however, we will lead with uncertainty and insecurity. This will trickle down to our people, too, and they will become focused on pleasing others rather than accomplishing the vision.

One of the most effective ways leaders can bless the people they serve with is to keep them focused on the great things that have happened in the past and the potential of the future, rather than simply raising up a bunch of people whose days are consumed with putting out fires.

EXCELLENT LEADERS ARE CONFIDENT

I struggle with confidence.

I was never a great athlete.

My performance in school did not garner the attention of colleges.

I've always had a hard time staying focused on one thing.

No one is more surprised about the success our church has experienced than I am!

As I've spoken with leaders both in the church and in the corporate world, I've discovered that I'm not alone in this battle for confidence. Almost every leader falls into seasons of discouragement, and if we don't put those doubts to rest, they can cripple us from moving forward.

When our confidence flags, the temptation is to resign, go somewhere else, and start all over. However, we always take our problems with us.

Every leader I know understands what it's like to allow pressure to rob us of confidence. Before long we find ourselves cowering, attempting to please as many people as possible.

However, several years ago, someone gave me a new perspective on pressure. He told me that pressure is God's call to humility in our lives. I'm beginning to understand that pressure brings more potential for progress than living on easy street does.

The leadership pressures I face drive me to the next verse in Psalm 23:

> Surely your goodness and love will follow me
>   all the days of my life,
> and I will dwell in the house of the LORD
>   forever.

PSALM 23:6

No matter how much pressure I'm experiencing, His love will follow me all the days of my life—even the bad ones.

In a world that highlights failures, flops, and fumbles, it's awesome to know that my circumstances don't alter God's character. He is still for me, and I can find my confidence in His presence, not in my own abilities.

After all David had been through, after everything he'd faced and the uncertainties life had thrown his way, he still had confidence in the Lord and His unchanging nature.

In other words, he was saying, "Even when I don't like my circumstances, I will trust Your character."

God's character is unchanging and solid—something we can anchor our souls to, knowing He won't change.

As leaders, we certainly aren't perfect or unchangeable like God is. But we can make it our passion and commitment to become more like Christ, pursuing honesty and integrity. After all, it's only when we have character that we can walk in true confidence. We don't have to be scared that people will find out what's really going on, because our leadership on the outside matches what's on the inside.

* * *

Average leaders work as hard as possible to make sure they're protected and positioned to go to the next level. Excellent leaders, however, make sure their people are protected. They do whatever it takes to put them in the best position to succeed.

QUESTIONS TO HELP YOU LEAD IN THE MOST EXCELLENT WAY

Questions to Ask Yourself

1. In which of these six areas do I need to grow the most: providing for my people, creating a healthy environment, giving guidance, being present, focusing on blessings, or being confident?
2. Do the people on my team have clear job descriptions? Do they know the expectations for their positions? When they mess up, do I take the time to point out what went wrong and coach them through it?
3. What actions can I take to create a culture in which my people feel protected?

Questions to Ask Your Team

1. Am I asking anything of you that I haven't given you the resources to carry out?
2. Is there anything about our work environment that impedes your ability to do your job well?

SUMMARY STATEMENTS

→ If you're going to be an excellent leader, you must be willing to protect the people who work with you.

→ People love working for leaders who fight for them rather than with them.

→ If God called you to it, He will see you through it.

→ Change of place + change of pace = change of perspective.

→ If we really love people, we won't let them get it wrong for very long.

→ Leaders who always protect make themselves more visible in tough times.

#BestWayToLead

CHAPTER 14

ALWAYS TRUSTS

Love . . . always trusts.
1 CORINTHIANS 13:6-7

IF BERNIE MADOFF were released from prison today, opened up an investment firm tomorrow, and asked you to be his first client, would you sign up?

Or let's say you had an opportunity to hire someone, but after a little research, you discovered they'd been released from their previous job because they'd stolen money. Would you be inclined to hire them?

If you had a meeting with someone where you shared something in confidence, only to find out later that the person had shared the information you'd asked them to keep private, would you tell that person confidential information in the future?

While I'm not the sharpest knife in the drawer, I'm guessing the answer to all of the above would be no!

When it comes to leadership, trust is a really big deal. Whether you lead a family of five, a church of seventy-five, or a company that makes $75 million a year, you have to be able to trust the people around you if you're going to excel in leadership.

Paul understood this concept: "Love . . . always trusts" (1 Corinthians 13:6-7).

A few years ago I went through a serious struggle with depression, to the point where I actually considered taking my own life. Through counseling, I discovered that one of the problems was that I felt like I had to do everything. I was a total control freak who didn't completely trust the people around me. That resulted in paralyzing pressure on me, as well as an unhealthy culture on my team.

After I identified this issue, I was able to begin loosening the reins I'd held on to so tightly. I knew that the leadership team in place around me was made up of brilliant men and women who loved the church we were serving, so why in the world would I think I couldn't trust them?

When I share with other leaders the importance of letting go of control and trusting their people, I get quite a bit of pushback. Some leaders say, "The people on my team don't do things the way I would." I share with them what a mentor said to me years ago, when I shared the same objection with him: "No one will ever do things 100 percent the way you would, but when you find someone who will do them in the 80 percent range, just leave the other 20 percent alone."

Although I am the leader, I recognize that I don't get things right 100 percent of the time. So when people approach things in a different way than I do, it's a chance for me to learn from those I lead.

People want to be trusted. All too often as leaders, we fall into the trap of delegating responsibility without also delegating the authority for someone to do what has been asked of them.

The reason we hold back delegating authority? A lack of trust.

One of the amazing things about Jesus' leadership was that even though He was perfect, He gave His imperfect disciples the authority to carry on His work. He gave them the authority to execute the vision and then followed up with instructions about how to do it.

We see an example of this in the book of Mark:

> Jesus went from village to village, teaching the people. And he called his twelve disciples together and began sending them out two by two, *giving them authority* to cast out evil spirits. He told them to take nothing for their journey except a walking stick—no food, no traveler's bag, no money. He allowed them to wear sandals but not to take a change of clothes.
>
> "Wherever you go," he said, "stay in the same house until you leave town. But if any place refuses to welcome you or listen to you, shake its dust from your feet as you leave to show that you have abandoned those people to their fate."
>
> MARK 6:6-11, NLT (EMPHASIS ADDED)

When we learn to trust the people who serve with us, our vision has the potential to grow beyond us. However, if we refuse to trust people and always come up with excuses to have our hands in everything, whatever we're leading will be limited to our own thoughts and ideas.

Excellent leaders aren't the ones who sign off on all the decisions; they're the ones with the responsibility to provide solid vision, set clear standards, and allow people to execute the tasks and assignments they've been given in the way that seems best to them.

If you don't have trustworthy people surrounding you, then you have the wrong people on your team.

Several years ago, I sat down with the leadership team at my church and shared with them nine filters to use whenever we're faced with a difficult decision. I believe these filters serve as both guardrails to protect the vision of our church and a framework to empower people to make decisions themselves, without having to run to me every time they have a question.

I hope these filters will be helpful for you and your organization as well. You may want to tweak them for your particular environment, but this list can get you started.

FILTER #1: WHAT DOES THE BIBLE SAY?

The first filter for us is Scripture. If someone wants to do something that is a clear violation of Scripture, then the answer is no.

For example, if someone is singing, goes for a high note, and misses it, no one is allowed to kill them after the song.

Or if someone makes you angry in a meeting and your go-to reaction is to leap across the table and use their face as a punching bag, that would be a pretty clear violation of Scripture. (However, it would be an incredible YouTube video!)

It may seem obvious for us as a church to use Scripture as a filter, but even if you're not in a church or ministry setting, you can still use this filter.

For example, let's say you've a signed contract with a business, and you begin to get word that the company may not be living up to their end of the deal.

In this scenario, lawyers are usually called, threats are made, and tensions run high. You might be tempted to see how you can wiggle out of the contract as quickly as possible.

However, Jesus once said to let your yes be yes and your no be no (see Matthew 5:37). This statement indicates that our commitment isn't predicated on the performance of another person.

And while we can't control how another person or company will respond, the ethical thing to do is to make our best attempt to fulfill our obligations in the contract.

Every day, you will face opportunities to do things the world's way or God's way. Be intentional as you make those calls.

FILTER #2: WHAT DO GODLY, WISE PEOPLE SAY?

When it comes to a decision that the Bible doesn't address specifically, the next filter to consider is what people we respect have to say about the situation.

Notice the filter is not "What do the people who think and see exactly the way I do say?" That type of mind-set is held by mediocre leaders who are afraid other people might have (and might be recognized for) an original idea. We need to be open to the input of a select group of people who will speak the truth to us in love.

Let's take another look at David's life.

One of the passions that captivated his heart as a leader was to bring the Ark of the Covenant back to the city of Jerusalem. The Ark was significant to the Israelites because it served as a symbol of the presence of God, but it had been captured by one of Israel's enemies and then neglected for some time.

David had a vision for that to change.

His vision was good; however, he went about fulfilling that vision in the wrong way. Scripture shows us the setup for a bad leadership move:

> David consulted with all his officials, including the
> generals and captains of his army. Then he addressed the
> entire assembly of Israel as follows: "If you approve and if

it is the will of the LORD our God, let us send messages to
all the Israelites throughout the land, including the priests
and Levites in their towns and pasturelands. Let us invite
them to come and join us. It is time to bring back the Ark
of our God, for we neglected it during the reign of Saul."

The whole assembly agreed to this, for the people
could see it was the right thing to do.

1 CHRONICLES 13:1-4, NLT

At first glance, this seems to be an excellent move for David—
in terms of both leadership and politics. It's clear from this passage
that he consulted with the military counsel around him, and the
opinion polls were strongly in his favor.

However, when it came to the specifics of dealing with the
Ark—specifically, the way it was to be carried—he failed to consult
the people who knew the details: the priests and Levites. These
religious leaders were informed about the decision but not asked
for their input.

A crew began transporting the Ark, and a huge celebration
ensued. But soon the party came to a screeching halt.

When they arrived at the threshing floor of Nacon, the
oxen stumbled, and Uzzah reached out his hand to steady
the Ark. Then the LORD's anger was aroused against
Uzzah, and he struck him dead because he had laid his
hand on the Ark. So Uzzah died there in the presence
of God.

1 CHRONICLES 13:9-10, NLT

You're welcome to your own interpretation here, but the way
I see it, David's decision to move the Ark without asking the right

people how to do it ultimately resulted in Uzzah losing his life. Naturally, this brought an end to the party (nothing like a guy being struck dead to ruin the mood!).

David was determined to bring the Ark to Jerusalem, and although he had the approval of nearly everyone, he failed miserably. But even in the wake of this misstep, David remained committed to fulfilling the vision the Lord had put on his heart. So he tried it again, but this time he consulted the people he should have talked to from the beginning.

> David now built several buildings for himself in the City of David. He also prepared a place for the Ark of God and set up a special tent for it. Then he commanded, "No one except the Levites may carry the Ark of God. The Lord has chosen them to carry the Ark of the Lord and to serve him forever."
>
> Then David summoned all Israel to Jerusalem to bring the Ark of the Lord to the place he had prepared for it. . . .
>
> Then David summoned the priests, Zadok and Abiathar, and these Levite leaders: Uriel, Asaiah, Joel, Shemaiah, Eliel, and Amminadab. He said to them, "You are the leaders of the Levite families. You must purify yourselves and all your fellow Levites, so you can bring the Ark of the Lord, the God of Israel, to the place I have prepared for it. Because you Levites did not carry the Ark the first time, the anger of the Lord our God burst out against us. We failed to ask God how to move it properly." So the priests and the Levites purified themselves in order to bring the Ark of the Lord, the

God of Israel, to Jerusalem. Then the Levites carried the
Ark of God on their shoulders with its carrying poles, just
as the LORD had instructed Moses.

I CHRONICLES 15:1-3, 11-15, NLT

This time David didn't just consult the people around him who
would rubber-stamp any idea he had; instead, he sought the advice
of those who were most qualified to make the decision. Since he
was secure enough to involve godly, wise people in what he was
trying to do, his vision was fulfilled.

When it's time to make plans for the student and children's
ministries in our church, I try not to make any big decisions without first getting the input of the staff who work in those areas.

When it comes to financial decisions, I won't make a decision
without asking for input from the staff members who lead our
financial department.

When it comes to songs and service programming, I don't like to
slam my hand down and declare, "This is the way it is!" Instead, I seek
those who are creatively gifted and get their thoughts and opinions.

As Scripture says, "Plans go wrong for lack of advice; many
advisers bring success" (Proverbs 15:22, NLT).

FILTER #3: WHAT DO MY PAST EXPERIENCES SAY?

A leadership mistake is truly bad only if a person keeps making the
same mistake over and over again.

One of the challenges our church faces is trying to accommodate the crowds that attend our Christmas and Easter services. We
often see double our average attendance for these events, and it can
be challenging to make sure we have adequate parking, seating, and
space in our children's ministry.

Several years ago, we discovered that some churches use tickets for their Christmas and Easter services, which allows them to make sure the crowds are evenly dispersed among the different service times.

I thought this was a great idea, so we decided to implement tickets at NewSpring for our upcoming Christmas services.

It went over like Vanilla Ice's rap career!

We didn't actually collect the tickets at the door, so people who brought their tickets were confused when they showed up.

Lots of people simply didn't attend church because they didn't have a ticket and were afraid they'd be turned away (even though we'd assured them they would still be welcome).

Some people tried to sell their tickets, which were free in the first place. (No, I'm not making that up!)

The ticket idea created more confusion and chaos than we ever anticipated.

When Easter rolled around, we decided to try the ticket system again, but this time we developed our plan more fully and explained it to the church more clearly.

This time there was even more chaos than there'd been at Christmas.

So we stopped doing tickets.

A year or so later, we were talking through the challenges of making sure the crowds received adequate care at our Christmas services when a new person on our staff piped up, "I know of this church that gives out tickets . . ."

We shot him on the spot.

Just kidding. But we did explain why this system may be effective in other settings but isn't a good fit for our church.

As it has often been said, "Those who don't learn from history are doomed to repeat it."

FILTER #4: WHAT DOES THE HOLY SPIRIT SAY?

Depending on your faith background, it might sound mysterious and even a little weird to you to think of the Holy Spirit guiding your decisions. But in reality, this is one of the smartest things you can do as a leader.

Before Jesus was crucified, He promised His disciples that they would receive the Holy Spirit: "The Advocate, the Holy Spirit, whom the Father will send in my name, will teach you all things and will remind you of everything I have said to you" (John 14:26).

Listening to the Holy Spirit is basically just asking God to give you the Spirit's wisdom—something like a spiritual gut check.

Let me be very clear in saying that I believe the Holy Spirit will never lead someone to do something contradictory to Scripture. I've seen tragic examples where leaders say they're "following the Spirit," but the aftermath of their decisions proves that they were just following their own desires.

When we ask God for guidance and the nudge we get from the Holy Spirit lines up with what Scripture says, we are in a position to be way more effective than we ever could have imagined.

When our church was just getting off the ground, we met in a room where we could squeeze in about 150 people max. We were doing two services and had completely outgrown our space.

Every time I prayed about it, I felt in my gut that we were supposed to move to a facility that would seat 1,100 people—a room that was on the same campus of the college where we were meeting.

It didn't make sense.

We didn't have the money.

We didn't have the people to fill the room.

But I couldn't shake the idea that this was the right decision.

People laughed at us and called us insane; however, within the span of about a year we had the funds and the people to make the move happen. After a year or so, about 1,600 people were attending on Sunday mornings. Without the prompting of the Holy Spirit, I never would have tried to move forward with this change.

Before I move on, let me beg you not to play the "Holy Spirit card" unless you're truly feeling led by the Lord. If you say, "God told me . . ." and you keep screwing things up, you'll eventually lose the trust of the people under your leadership.

FILTER #5: DOES THIS NEGATIVELY IMPACT OUR VISION?

You may find this difficult to believe, but I'm an extremely opinionated person. That's true when it comes to sports, food, and politics.

At NewSpring, I often talk about sports and food. Politics, however, is a subject I stay away from. It's simply not the mission of our church to change the political atmosphere of our nation. Morality can't be legislated, and change comes about not as the result of laws changing but rather as the result of Jesus changing hearts.

Several years ago, we invited a popular speaker to our church to share his incredible story. We were all really excited as we anticipated this day.

But then the bottom fell out.

The organization this person was representing called and asked if they could distribute voters' guides to everyone who attended our campuses. I said no and tried to give a clear explanation for why this wasn't an option for us.

Would it have been a sin to distribute voters' guides to the church?

Nope. However, it would have negatively impacted our vision. We recognize that politics is a deeply divisive issue, and we don't want to isolate people immediately when they walk in the door. If something is going to offend them, we want to make sure it's the gospel, not a set of step-by-step instructions outlining who to vote for.

The organization said they understood; however, they called the next day to see if it would be possible to have people in the lobby passing out the guides to whoever wanted one.

Once again, I said no and explained that this wasn't in the framework of our vision.

The next week they called and asked if they could put a "political information piece" on each chair in the church. It wouldn't necessarily declare who to vote for but would simply tell the facts.

At this point, I had to make the difficult decision to cancel the speaker. It was clear that he was trying to make a point that would isolate people I really cared about reaching. Since this visit would have negatively impacted our vision, I had to say no to someone who was not happy with me at all.

If an organization compromises its vision, it eventually becomes a place where the main goal is to keep everyone happy rather than to actually move forward toward the bigger goal.

FILTER #6: IS THIS SOMETHING WE CAN GENUINELY BE EXCITED ABOUT?

NewSpring has more than four hundred staff members, and with such a large employee roster, one of the challenges we face on a consistent basis is communication.

Here are just a few examples of things that could go wrong due to a lack of communication: A programming decision is made, but the campus pastors aren't aware of it. A staff member gets moved from one job to another, and people find out about it three months later. Someone on staff is let go, and the staff hears the news from Facebook instead of from the church leaders.

After new employees have been on staff at NewSpring for three months, they are asked to fill out an evaluation form about the work environment.

It didn't take me long to notice that communication was an area that a number of people felt could be improved, so our leadership team decided to make a conscious effort to deal with this.

We discovered that we were relying on a system that had been effective when we had forty people but simply didn't work well with four hundred.

It was the famous all-staff e-mail.

Our system was to send out an e-mail to the entire staff once a week that communicated the essentials everyone needed to be aware of. Just about anyone could request that something be put in an all-staff e-mail, and we eventually got to the point where these messages were so large your computer would explode if you tried to download one.

As the leadership team was meeting about this issue and trying to figure out how to get the staff to read the volumes of material we were sending every week, a thought dawned on me: *I don't read the staff e-mail.* In fact, I would have rather had someone set a fire on my head and put it out with a sledgehammer than make my way through one of those.

I stopped the meeting and asked, "Does anyone in the room actually read the all-staff e-mail every week?"

No one raised their hand. *No one!*

We decided right then and there that we weren't going to try to communicate any type of excitement and information through an avenue we weren't excited about ourselves.

This led us to discover more effective ways to get the right information into everyone's hands.

As leaders, we can't expect our team to get behind something we're not excited about ourselves. Doing so leads us to being fake, which always comes back to bite us.

FILTER #7: IS THIS A TEMPORARY SOLUTION?

One of the pieces of advice I often give the people I serve with is "Please don't put a Band-Aid on a bullet wound."

Being a leader is hard—especially when it means making unpopular, gut-wrenching decisions. If we're not careful, we'll end up opting for the easy decision rather than the right decision.

I recall a painful period for me as a leader when we experienced rapid turnover in a particular area of our team. The transition was difficult and resulted in a lot of people (including me) having to step up and cover for positions that had been left vacant.

During this time, I made some hiring decisions simply to stop the bleeding. This meant everyone could catch their breath temporarily, but these quick fixes caused more pain in the long term. One of the key hires had to be released less than six weeks later because he simply wasn't the right person for the job.

I can tell you from experience that the temporary relief from pain isn't worth the deeper challenges caused by making a decision that's not best in the broader scope of the organization.

FILTER #8: IS THIS EXCELLENCE OR EXTRAVAGANCE?

As followers of Christ, we should have the highest standards of excellence in the world. After all, we follow Someone who never offered anything less than His very best for us, so why would we offer Him a lame effort and then say it's all for His glory?

So while we should always try to put forth our best effort in our business or church or family, there are two things we should keep in mind for perspective.

First, excellence is *not* perfection; rather, it's simply doing our best with what we've been given.

Second, extravagance doesn't always equal excellence.

When someone is consistently saying that the answer to their problem is more staff and more money, they're identifying themselves as noncreative leaders who are unwilling to do whatever it takes to execute the vision.

Don't get me wrong—there are times to add people and increase budgets; however, making a newer, shinier car is meaningless if the engine keeps breaking down.

I don't want our team to think "more resources" every time they see a problem; rather, I want them to think "more opportunities"—more opportunities to be creative and to be great stewards of all that's been placed in our hands.

FILTER #9: WILL THIS BENEFIT THE BROADER VISION OR YOUR PERSONAL VISION?

Beware of the person who always has to be the leading scorer on the team.

Our vision at NewSpring Church is to reach people who are far from God and teach them how to follow Jesus step-by-step.

Every person and every department knows this.

It's something we come back to over and over again—and something our entire staff is dedicated to.

But it would be difficult to get everyone on board with the vision if I didn't believe in it myself. This filter must be used by the senior leader before it can be passed down to other people on staff.

Here are some questions to ask yourself to gauge your commitment to the larger vision:

- Am I making leadership decisions based on what's best for me or what's best for everyone?
- Am I asking people to do things I would be unwilling to do myself?
- Do I care about people because of what they can do for me?

There is hardly anything more destructive than leaders who want to use people or a company or a church to get their name out and achieve as much personal gain as possible.

This attitude will destroy the culture of an organization. People will end up feeling used and abused, and it won't be long before the sharpest employees leave. Excellent leaders are the ones who are more passionate about the cause of the organization than their own reputations.

*   *   *

Ever since I shared these filters with my team, we've seen our effectiveness and buy-in across the entire staff increase. We've seen the old adage "People are more likely to buy in after they have weighed in" turn out to be true.

If these filters will work for your organization, please take them and use them. If not, develop your own. Either way, the goal is to get to the point where you can completely trust the people on your team.

When we have a foundation of trust, we can accomplish more together than we ever could on our own.

QUESTIONS TO HELP YOU LEAD IN THE MOST EXCELLENT WAY

Questions to Ask Yourself

1. Have I set my team up to make excellent decisions without me?
2. Are there any areas where I need to let go of control?

Questions to Ask Your Team

1. Do you feel like I've given you the authority to carry out the responsibilities you've been given?
2. What are some ways we could build more trust on our team?

SUMMARY STATEMENTS

→ When we learn to trust the people who serve with us, our vision has the potential to grow beyond us.

→ A leadership mistake is truly bad only if a person keeps making the same mistake over and over again.

→ If an organization compromises its vision, it becomes a place where the goal is to keep everyone happy rather than to move forward.

→ Excellence is *not* perfection; rather, it's simply doing our best with what we've been given.

→ Excellent leaders are more passionate about the cause of the organization than their own reputations.

#BestWayToLead

CHAPTER 15

ALWAYS HOPES

Love . . . always hopes.

1 CORINTHIANS 13:6-7

ONE OF THE SCARIEST DAYS of my life occurred fifteen years ago, on an otherwise ordinary Thursday evening.

NewSpring was about three months old, and things were going better than we could have ever imagined in every area. Every area, that is, except giving.

At the time, 80 percent of our church was made up of college students, which was incredible in regard to energy but horrible in regard to making a budget, since most of them were so broke that when they went to McDonald's, they had to put their milk shakes on layaway!

Our weekly offerings allowed us to meet our most basic needs and have a few hundred dollars in the bank in case an emergency developed, but that was about it.

I remember checking the mail that Thursday (the church's mail came to my personal PO box) and noticing an unfamiliar envelope. I opened it to discover a bill for $1,500. I just about messed my pants on the spot.

We did not have $1,500.

No one in the church had $1,500.

We were not even taking in $1,500 a week.

I went home and called the person who had sent the bill, reminding him that per our earlier arrangement, we'd have extended time to make the payment. He didn't recall that particular conversation (which is the moment I learned to get everything in writing) and said the bill was due in thirty days.

I would love to tell you that I was as solid as a rock, that I didn't doubt for a minute something great was going to happen. I would like to tell you I went on my way with a bounce in my step and a song in my heart, but that would be a lie.

For the next several days, I went from freaking out to wanting to quit. I'm ashamed to admit this now, but during that time I lost every ounce of hope I'd previously had. A sense of darkness crept in, and it was scary and painful.

I kept this problem to myself, which caused me to feel not only hopeless but also isolated. I began to allow imaginary doomsday scenarios to dominate my thinking, and I actually considered giving up on the idea of NewSpring altogether.

The following Sunday I delivered a less-than-stellar message. Afterward I was standing around carrying on conversations with people when a guy who had been a part of the church for a while approached me.

He stood there rather awkwardly for a minute and then approached me like he was about to tell me a secret. "Um, can I speak with you in private?"

When we were off to the side of the room, he said, "Hey, man, I don't want you to tell anyone about this, but this week at work I got a bonus I wasn't expecting at all. As I prayed about it, I really felt like Jesus told me to give it to NewSpring."

I was filled with gratitude and immediately thought this might be a way to make a dent in the bill I'd received just a few days before.

"If you don't mind my asking, how much was the bonus?" I asked.

"Fifteen hundred dollars," he said.

I nearly messed my pants again.

I've never forgotten that event. All sorts of lessons can be gained from that experience, but the one that has always remained at the top of my mind is how important it is for a leader to have hope.

Hope is one of the most powerful tools available to us.

Hope is what keeps us going when everyone else is ready to give up.

Hope is what causes us to believe that our setbacks are merely setups for greater things than we could ever imagine.

Hope is what allows a leader to stand firm when everyone else is running scared.

Hope is also one of the marks of an excellent leader: "Love . . . always hopes" (1 Corinthians 13:6-7).

David, an excellent leader himself, made this request of God: "Lead me by your truth and teach me, for you are the God who saves me. All day long I put my hope in you" (Psalm 25:5, NLT).

Over and over again in the psalms, David declared his hope in God through less than hopeful circumstances.

In the business world, there are a number of different job titles for leaders:

- CEO: chief executive officer
- CFO: chief financial officer
- COO: chief operating officer
- CCCO: chief Candy Crush officer (just seeing if you're still with me!)

These positions are important, and each one plays a crucial role in an organization. However, I think every leader on the planet, regardless of their title, should be a CHO—a chief hope officer. We have a choice: will we be fueled by hope or dragged down by circumstances?

Given the choice, I choose hope.

I should warn you, however, that hope doesn't always come easily. Having been in some sort of leadership position for more than twenty years, I've learned there's hardly anything more vulnerable than allowing yourself to hope for something.

One phone call, e-mail, or text can erase our hope and replace it with bitterness and uncertainty. When we begin to lead out of bitterness and uncertainty rather than hope, we become discouraged, visionless leaders—the kind no one wants to be around.

So how do we lead with hope and guard the hope inside us? In my view, we need to be aware of four "hope busters" that come after all of us at some point.

HOPE BUSTER #1: MANUFACTURING ENERGY

As everyone who attends NewSpring or follows me on social media knows, I'm always telling our church that the next series (or the next sermon) is "the best thing we've ever done." I've been called the "hype guy" by some who think there's no way every Sunday can be the best. My reply to these naysayers has always been, "It's only hype if you don't believe it."

Recently I was in a Q&A session when someone asked, "What's your favorite sermon you've ever preached?"

Without hesitation I replied, "I haven't preached it yet."

What compelled me to give an answer like that? Hope!

I've been asked, "Isn't hope simply absurd optimism?"

My reply: "You're asking the wrong person, because I believe an optimist is someone who has the faith to take God at His word and trust Him even when circumstances scream otherwise!"

I have hope for the church I'm a part of, hope for the people I lead, and hope for the future that's coming our way.

However, if I ever get to the point where I'm manufacturing energy (pretending to be excited about something), hope will seep out of me like helium from a week-old balloon.

This happened to me in February 2006, when we moved from a portable location to a brand-new, permanent facility.

Since the building we'd rented for six years was used for other purposes, we were only able to do services and activities on Sundays. When we moved into our new facility, we suddenly had the option of using the building whenever we wanted to. A lot of churches in the southeastern part of the United States have a midweek service that's a little more insider focused. Our staff agreed that we didn't want to do a service every week, but we'd heard of churches that did a midweek service once a month on the first Wednesday, so we followed suit and called the event "First Wednesday."

On those evenings, our church would meet and sing, and I would preach. Everyone loved it.

Except the volunteers and staff.

The longer we continued the program, the tougher it became to maintain our excitement. I remember saying on a Sunday, "Hey, y'all, I am so excited about First Wednesday this week." Meanwhile, I was thinking, *Oh my gosh, I just lied to my entire church! I'm not excited about First Wednesday; in fact, I wish Jesus would come back before Wednesday so we wouldn't have to do the stupid service.*

The next day I expressed my unfiltered thoughts in a leadership team meeting and was surprised that everyone else agreed. I asked them to survey their staff and key volunteers about the midweek service. They all came back with the same response: "We're pretending to be excited about something none of us want to do."

We didn't cut the program immediately. The next First Wednesday, I noticed that my attitude was horrible, the staff was walking around with slumped shoulders, and key volunteers looked like they'd rather be in a chow line in prison.

We were telling people to show up and promising them it would be the most exciting experience on the planet, yet none of the staff would have attended if they hadn't been paid to be there.

The next month we decided to stop First Wednesdays.

On paper, this decision didn't make sense. More than two thousand people were showing up nearly every time we opened the doors, but our leadership team believed integrity was more important than having a huge crowd at a midweek service.

After making this decision, I noticed an obvious change in our culture. It was then I decided I would never say I'm excited about something that I'm not excited about. This commitment has helped ensure that my hope bucket stays full, and it allows me to be the CHO in our church.

HOPE BUSTER #2: SUSPICION

I have a really awesome joke I like to play on people. (You should try this!)

When I have a passenger or a group of people in my car and I'm backing out of a parking space, I roll down my window. Once everyone is talking away, I slam on the brakes and hit the outside of my car really hard with my hand.

It sounds (and feels) like I've just hit something.

I've had people scream, cuss, spill things, and nearly pass out. It really is hilarious, and I plan on doing it forever.

However, once someone has gone through this experience as my passenger, they are always suspicious of me when I roll down my window.

Always!

Even if I'm driving down the interstate at seventy-five miles per hour, if I roll down my window, they'll stop whatever they're doing to watch me.

Because of this "innocent" pastime, people just don't trust me in certain situations when I'm behind the wheel.

This may be funny when it comes to cars, but it's pretty serious when it comes to people. It's impossible for us to hope in a person and for a person when we're suspicious of their motives.

I should mention here that there are times when it's appropriate not to be hopeful about someone. If a person has consistently dropped the ball or is always the center of controversy, or if you've just healed from the last time they stabbed you in the back, it's wise to put up some boundaries to protect yourself from being let down or hurt again. However, if you are "naturally skeptical" about everyone on your team, you need to take stock of your leadership style. A lack of hope in your people will limit their ability to excel under your leadership.

King Saul was always suspicious of David, even though David had never given him a reason to be. This lack of hope in David was rooted in Saul's deep insecurity. The same is true for leaders today. Our insecurities can put a lid on our success if we don't figure out a way to battle through them.

Jesus said it best in the Golden Rule: "Do to others as you would like them to do to you" (Luke 6:31, NLT). In other words, we should treat people the way we would want to be treated. Even if you aren't a Christian, you have to agree that's some great advice.

My friend Andy Stanley says that when it comes to people and circumstances, there's a gap between what we know and what we don't know. We get to choose what we want to fill that gap with—we can fill it with either trust or suspicion. When other people have a gap about us, we want them to fill it with trust—to give us the benefit of the doubt. Jesus was saying that if this is the kind of treatment we want to receive from others, that's what we should be willing to give to them.

When it comes to leading people, love always assumes the best.

Not only is suspicion a miserable way to live, it also holds us back from empowering those around us to become what they were intended to be.

HOPE BUSTER #3: LACK OF VISION

My eye doctor was examining my eyes during a routine visit when I heard him say, "Uh-oh!"

Let's be honest: no one wants to hear any doctor say, "Uh-oh!" So I asked him to please explain.

"Perry, I was hoping we were several years away from this conversation, but due to what I'm seeing right now, it's time for you to step into what we call progressive lenses."

I was okay with that until he explained to me that "progressive lenses" is basically the politically correct term for bifocals.

After a stunned silence, I finally managed to ask, "Why is this necessary?"

He explained that over time, a person's eyesight diminishes—some faster than others—and mine was declining at record-breaking speed.

As I sat in my living room that night, I kept thinking about my experience with the eye doctor and how it had implications for leaders, too. If we aren't strategic and intentional, our vision will diminish over time, until one day we wake up and our biggest desire is simply to make it back to bed as soon as possible.

A lack of vision will lead to a lack of passion. And once leaders lose their passion, chances are this apathy will be contagious across the organization.

I've heard vision described in several ways. One of my friends describes it as "painting a picture that produces passion in people." Another friend says it's "describing things as they could be and should be." Here's the definition I've come up with over the years: "that thing" you have inside you that compels you to attempt things that stretch you, ignite a white-hot passion in you, and benefit more people than just you.

Whatever our vision is, we have to make sure it's deeply anchored in our souls before we can attempt to export it to someone else.

A great vision is not "I am incredibly undisciplined, hate authority, and feel utterly bored, but I have a great idea." Rather, it's "I have a white-hot passion inside me to make a difference, and I feel like I'm going to explode if I don't figure out how to make this become a reality."

I have to keep the vision in front of me every day; if not, I find myself just going through the motions. Nothing robs people of hope as much as when their work is driven more by routine than imagination.

One day after work, I walked out of my office, got into my car, and headed home. The next thing I remember, I was sitting in my driveway. I had zoned out the entire way home. I hadn't been drinking. I hadn't popped any pills. I had simply become so familiar with the drive that it didn't require me to engage mentally to make it to my destination.

The same thing can happen to us if we don't keep the vision in front of us. We'll drive the familiar routes on autopilot, and doing so will create an environment where mediocrity is the unspoken core value. Instead of striving together toward a worthy goal, people simply hope for five o'clock to arrive as soon as possible.

An organization where people are just clocking in may pay a decent salary, but it has zero potential to change the world.

We can't wrap up this discussion without talking about God's vision for His people. As your vision of God increases, so will your vision of what He wants to do in and through you. Once you've gotten a glimpse of who God is, I guarantee you won't be compelled to pursue "average."

I believe that the main leadership problem in Western culture isn't a resource problem; it's a vision problem. If we as leaders will fix our eyes on Jesus, see people as He sees them, lead the way He leads, and believe He will do what Scripture says He'll do, we will see modern-day miracles that will blow our minds.

Jesus Himself said, "I tell you the truth, anyone who believes in me will do the same works I have done, and even greater works, because I am going to be with the Father" (John 14:12, NLT).

If you are feeling discouraged and tempted to throw up your hands right now because your budget has been slashed, your employees are apathetic, church attendance in our country is decreasing, or Christians are being marginalized, I'd like to give you this assurance: there is still hope.

God loves the underdog! If you don't believe me, let me remind you of the story about a boy named David who fought the giant Goliath.

HOPE BUSTER #4: LACK OF DISCIPLINE

I used to be fat!

I know *fat* is not a politically correct term and some people are offended by it. However, understand that I'm talking about myself here. I was not "fluffy"; I was not "big boned." I was buffet-busting, soda pop–drinking, ice cream–slurping fat.

Honestly, I didn't enjoy it. Eating too much food was a drug for me—a vice that seemed impossible to escape. I can still remember the names I was called on the playground by kids in elementary school.

Because of my lack of discipline when it came to food, I weighed around three hundred pounds and wore a size fifty in the waist . . . in the ninth grade!

I had no hope of getting a date, wearing anything fashionable, or feeling good about myself.

One day I was sitting on my living room couch and decided I simply was not going to live that way anymore. I'm not sure how to explain the change, but something inside me just snapped. I went for a run (a very short one, I should add), and suddenly I was on fire to become healthier.

Over the next year, I lost fourteen inches in my waist and dropped more than eighty pounds. Ever since, people have asked me, "What's the main thing you did to lose weight?"

My answer is the one no one wants to hear: "Discipline."

All too often, people want things they're unwilling to work for.

Wanting something great for yourself, your company, or your church isn't a bad thing; in fact, it can be the fuel that sets your heart on fire. However, what holds people back from achieving their potential isn't usually a lack of vision; rather, it's a lack of execution.

As discipline increases, so does our progress. And as progress increases, so does our hope.

One of the most well-known miracles in the Bible is when Jesus turned water into wine.

The next day there was a wedding celebration in the village of Cana in Galilee. Jesus' mother was there, and Jesus and his disciples were also invited to the celebration. The wine supply ran out during the festivities, so Jesus' mother told him, "They have no more wine."

"Dear woman, that's not our problem," Jesus replied. "My time has not yet come."

But his mother told the servants, "Do whatever he tells you."

Standing nearby were six stone water jars, used for Jewish ceremonial washing. Each could hold twenty to thirty gallons. Jesus told the servants, "Fill the jars with water." When the jars had been filled, he said, "Now dip some out, and take it to the master of ceremonies." So the servants followed his instructions.

JOHN 2:1-8, NLT

This beverage shortage was a huge cultural boo-boo! Whoever planned the wedding didn't arrange for there to be enough wine. We don't know if the wedding planners were trying to save money or if everyone had gotten so hammered they were speaking in cursive, but what we do know is that they were out of wine, and Jesus was presented with the problem.

Instead of waving His hand and making wine appear (which I'm confident He could have done), He asked the servants to fill six jars with water. Now let this detail sink in: each one could hold up to thirty gallons of water.

This observation never really hit me until recently, when I had to fill up a two-gallon bucket. I stuck the bucket in the sink, turned on the water, and waited. And waited . . . and waited. It seemed to take forever.

As I was waiting, I recalled this story. *They didn't have a water faucet to turn on—they most likely had to draw it from a well,* I thought.

So let's say there was a well outside and the bucket the servants used could hold a gallon of water. If that were the case, the servants would have had to drop the bucket into the well and pour it into the jars at least 120 times.

Do you think the servants thought Jesus was crazy at any point in this process? (I would have!)

Do you think they considered giving up?

Do you think they asked each other, "What's the point?"

We don't know what conversations they may have had, but we do know about the miracle that took place afterward. Jesus took their hard work and discipline and used it as a platform for a miracle.

Many times we as leaders lack the discipline to do what we need to do, because we don't see immediate results.

The difference between good and great organizations is the amount of preparation people are willing to put in to get the job done.

* * *

If you are feeling discouraged in your leadership right now, I'd like to encourage you to choose hope.

Hope allows us to hang on when everyone says to let go.

Hope compels us to believe in someone everyone else has given up on.

Hope fuels the passion that keeps us going when circumstances seem to be stacked against us.

And hope is the difference between a good leader and an excellent one.

QUESTIONS TO HELP YOU LEAD IN THE MOST EXCELLENT WAY

Questions to Ask Yourself

1. Is there any vision I'm owning that I don't believe in?
2. Is my default to trust people or to be suspicious of them? What impact does this tendency have on my leadership?

Questions to Ask Your Team

1. When I talk about the vision of our organization, does it produce excitement or fear in you?
2. What is our organization currently doing that we all wish we would stop doing? What are we not doing that we need to start?

SUMMARY STATEMENTS

→ We have a choice: Will we be fueled by hope or dragged down by circumstances?

→ Hope compels us to believe in someone everyone else has given up on.

→ When it comes to leading people, love always assumes the best.

→ Suspicion holds us back from empowering those around us to become who they were intended to be.

→ What holds people back from achieving their potential isn't usually a lack of vision; it's a lack of execution.

#BestWayToLead

CHAPTER 16

ALWAYS PERSEVERES

Love . . . always perseveres.
I CORINTHIANS 13:6-7

I MET A SEVEN-YEAR-OLD KID the other day who could list every single US president from memory.

Honestly, if you offered me one hundred dollars to name fifteen, I think your money would be safe.

The one president at the top of nearly everyone's list, however, is Abraham Lincoln.

I remember studying him in the second grade and being fascinated by all the challenges he overcame. (I also remember reading that he was from Indiana, but I misread it and thought he was from India. This led to a huge argument with my parents about his origins.)

When you consider all that he had to deal with as a leader, the list is pretty overwhelming:

- In 1832, he lost his job and was defeated for state legislature.
- In 1833, his business failed.

- In 1835, his sweetheart died.
- In 1836, he had a nervous breakdown.
- In 1838, he was defeated for Speaker of the House in Illinois.
- In 1843, he lost in his nomination bid for Congress.
- In 1855, he was defeated for US Senate.
- In 1856, he lost in his nomination bid for vice president.
- In 1858, he was again defeated for US Senate.
- In 1860, he was elected president of the United States.

Talk about a guy who wouldn't give up—a guy who fought through hard times and eventually left a legacy that impacted the world!

When I was growing up, I loved watching Michael Jordan play basketball. I will never forget watching a commercial where he said, "I've missed more than nine thousand shots in my career. I've lost almost three hundred games. Twenty-six times, I've been trusted to take the game-winning shot and missed. I've failed over and over and over again in my life. And that is why I succeed."

It doesn't matter if you loved him or hated him—the guy knew how to fight through adversity and persevere.

Let's dive back into Scripture for an epic example of perseverance. David knew a lot about fighting through tough times.

- He was a shepherd from an early age—a job that required him to fend off and kill a lion and a bear that had attacked his sheep.
- He had to fight against a giant who looked impossible to defeat—a battle no one else was willing to engage in.
- His success brought him persecution and nearly cost him his life at the hands of a jealous, insecure leader.
- He was promised a palace but instead spent years in caves, running from those who were out to harm him.

- He had family problems, including having a son who tried to kill him and take over the kingdom.

In spite of all this, David is considered one of the greatest leaders of all time.

It's not that excellent leaders never experience tough times; rather, they're able to persevere through them.

Every leader will endure hardship of some variety. The vision the Lord gives us is in direct proportion to the pain we are personally able to endure. I believe this is why Paul includes perseverance in his list of excellent leadership qualities: Love . . . always perseveres" (1 Corinthians 13:6-7).

Sometimes we see hard times coming, and even though we think we're prepared for them, they still overwhelm us. Other times challenges seem to come from out of nowhere.

A few years ago I took my daughter, Charisse, to the zoo. We were having a great time and were laughing about something we'd just seen, when all of a sudden a huge rock hit me on the side of my face.

The impact stunned me, and I was dazed for about five seconds or so. I looked around to see what in the world was going on. About five feet from me, I saw a little boy holding a rock in one hand. *Stupid kid,* I thought. *You should have at least put down the other rock so it wouldn't be so obvious you're guilty!*

I didn't really know what to do, so I asked, "Did you hit me in the head with that rock?"

He nodded.

"Where are your parents?"

He pointed to an older lady. "That's my grandma!"

I walked him over to her and explained what had happened, and she proceeded to whoop his rear end!

My trip to the zoo wasn't that different from what happens in leadership. There are days when we're going along and everything is awesome, and then *wham*—from out of nowhere, we get hit in the head and knocked loopy for a while.

A rock or two every once in a while isn't that big of a deal; however, when they all come at one time, it makes even the toughest leaders want to give up.

There's a story in the book of Acts that highlights this point. First, let me give you a little background: the apostle Paul, one of the main characters in the New Testament, was compelled by a vision to reach as many non-Jewish people as possible with the message of the gospel.

This wasn't just a good idea for him; it was an obsession he was willing to give his life for. (Side note: only people who are willing to put all they've got on the line to fulfill their passion make a difference.)

Paul went to Lystra, and at first he experienced success there. However, things soon took a really bad turn: "Some Jews arrived from Antioch and Iconium and won the crowds to their side. They stoned Paul and dragged him out of town, thinking he was dead" (Acts 14:19, NLT).

Talk about a bad day! As rock after rock got thrown at him, Paul probably thought this was it and he was on his way out.

You've probably felt that way as well. Although there are many challenges that may threaten to wear us down, here are three common "rocks" that often come our way as leaders.

PERSEVERANCE CHALLENGE #1: DISTRACTION

We all know what it's like to get sidetracked by distractions.

I'm not talking about the distractions we purposefully place in our lives (like checking our phone every five minutes just in case someone posted a picture that we need to "like" or make a comment about).

I'm talking about the distractions that really blindside us.

Someone who has been on your team for a long time lets you know they're moving on.

A misunderstanding takes place in the office—lines have been drawn, and people are choosing sides.

The budget isn't being met, which means expenses have to be cut.

I could go on, but you get the point.

In times like these, we are tempted to find a new company or church or group, or pursue a different career altogether. If we allow our minds to wander for too long, we can convince ourselves that anything is better than the situation we're currently in.

Several years ago, after I preached a horrible message, I told my wife, Lucretia, that I wanted to quit. "I'm going to apply for a job at Home Depot and stack lumber for the rest of my life," I said.

She smiled at me. "You would hate it, because you've been called to lead."

Excellent leaders don't allow distractions to destroy them. It's not easy, but as leaders, we are responsible for handling the big deals in such a way that they don't become really big deals again.

PERSEVERANCE CHALLENGE #2: DECEPTION

The second rock that seems to fly at leaders regularly is deception. Leaders often wrestle with the lie that they always have to have the right answers, that they're never allowed to have a bad day, and that they should work eighty-five hours a week to get everything done.

These expectations sometimes come from other people, but more often than not, they're pressures we put on ourselves out of fear and insecurity. We're afraid that if we don't know what to do, someone else will, and if other people get attention, we'll lose our positions. This is ultimately counterproductive because it leads us to attack people rather than the real problem. (Think of Saul hurling spears at David!)

Leaders who have to appear like they have it all together will eventually fall apart, because no one is called to lead in a state of isolation.

Let me be clear: solitude is an awesome thing. Solitude is when we take some time away from our normal rituals and routines and allow the break to refresh our thinking and recharge our batteries.

Isolation, however, is deadly. Unlike solitude, where we choose to be away temporarily, isolation occurs when we feel like we have to be away because no one understands us.

I've discovered that when I say, "No one understands me," it's no one's fault but my own. It's nothing more than an excuse for me to remain in a state of fear and uncertainty.

The way to overcome these deceptions is to open up and admit we don't have all the answers and we're overwhelmed. The people who follow will see this transparency not as a sign of weakness but as a sign of strength.

PERSEVERANCE CHALLENGE #3: DISCOURAGEMENT

There isn't a leader on the planet who doesn't have to deal with discouragement.

Sometimes discouragement comes in the form of a tsunami that crashes over us. Other times it's one small wave after another that erodes away our confidence. Either way, discouragement is a serious challenge every leader faces.

A few years ago, I had one of those days when it seemed like everything was going wrong. After a series of mishaps, one after another, I finally said out loud, "If one more thing goes wrong today, I'm going to snap!"

I snapped!

I sat on my back porch, staring into the woods and wondering if I should even go to work the next day.

I should pause here and mention that there were a lot of things going right at the time. The church was growing beyond all my expectations; I was married to a beautiful woman; we had just had Charisse, our amazing daughter; we had zero debt (other than our house); and I had the greatest staff in the world (still do). But when those rocks all hit me in the same day, I became convinced I needed to quit.

It's amazing how the little pebbles of discouragement can threaten to shake our perseverance.

As we continue with Paul's story, we see how he guarded against discouragement in his leadership: "As the believers gathered around him, he got up and went back into the town. The next day he left with Barnabas for Derbe" (Acts 14:20, NLT).

Paul didn't do his work alone. He had a team of people who worked with him to accomplish a vision that was larger than he could have carried out on his own.

Paul had plenty of reasons to be discouraged. For one thing, he got stoned, which essentially means people threw rocks at him until they thought he was dead. However, when his team gathered around him, he got up (notice that he wasn't picked up; he got up). Then he went back to the place where he'd just been pelted with rocks.

One of the things that enables us to persevere is the people we've surrounded ourselves with. Excellent leaders persevere because they're not trying to go it alone.

One of my greatest joys as a leader is having the privilege

of working with a team of people who really care about me as a person and will stand with me no matter what I'm going through.

When I was in the middle of a tough time recently, I had a friend tell me that "the purest gold comes out of the hottest fire." My friend was right: in times that call for perseverance, we can either run from the fire or be refined by it.

Pressure is simply a reminder to us that we need God and other people. It's a call to humility, not an indication that it's time to give up.

Another factor that motivates me to persevere is that one day, when my life on earth is over, I will stand before Jesus Christ, and He will look me in the eye. This is a Man whose assignment was much tougher than mine will ever be. He experienced abandonment, criticism, torture, and ultimately a cross. He could have quit at any time, but He didn't. He persevered, and because He didn't give up, I don't have to either.

What you see as an obstacle is most likely an opportunity to trust God, trust others, and walk in faith, knowing that in Christ, the best is always yet to come!

QUESTIONS TO HELP YOU LEAD IN THE MOST EXCELLENT WAY

Questions to Ask Yourself

1. Have I considered quitting recently? If so, why?
2. If I quit right now, will this be a story I'm proud of or a regret I'll carry for the rest of my life?
3. Do I have the right people around me—people who will stick with me no matter the circumstances?

Questions to Ask Your Team

1. Are there any lies we're believing as an organization? How can we do a better job speaking the truth to each other?
2. Are any of you discouraged to the point of wanting to quit? If so, is there anything that would change your mind?

SUMMARY STATEMENTS

→ It's not that excellent leaders never experience tough times; rather, they're able to persevere through them.

→ Only people who are willing to put all they've got on the line to fulfill their passion make a difference.

→ Excellent leaders persevere because they're not trying to go it alone.

→ In times that call for perseverance, we can either run from the fire or be refined by it.

→ What you see as an obstacle is most likely an opportunity to trust God, trust others, and walk in faith.

#BestWayToLead

NEVER FAILS

Love never fails.

1 CORINTHIANS 13:8

IT'S ONE OF THE QUESTIONS I'm asked most frequently in leadership circles: "Who is the greatest leader you've ever met?"

I've had the privilege of meeting some of the greatest leaders in the world—men and women who are having a profound impact on the lives of thousands of people. So when people ask me this question, I have a hunch they're expecting me to drop names and talk about sitting at the feet of a renowned leader as they poured principles into me like Yoda did for Luke Skywalker.

However, the greatest leader I've ever known is someone you have most likely never heard of.

Her name is Helen Noble.

Helen was never a president. She wasn't a CEO. She wasn't the head of a big nonprofit or the pastor of a megachurch.

Helen was my mother.

I had the privilege of knowing her for only twelve years, but the way she led me during that time has profoundly shaped the way I see life and leadership. Her life is proof that leadership isn't about the position you hold but rather the person you are.

I'll never forget the day I found out my mother had cancer.

She was scheduled for a routine operation to have her gall-bladder removed, but when the doctors began the procedure, they discovered that cancer had covered the inside of her body.

When the school bus dropped me off that day, I walked up to the house and was surprised to see several cars in the driveway.

My dad was inside. He'd been waiting until I got home to share the news with several family members who had gathered there.

"The doctors found cancer," he said. "They said it's too late. She'll most likely never come home from the hospital, since she needs constant medical attention."

I ran into the woods behind our house and cried for what seemed like hours.

I remember thinking, *If this is what God is like, I want nothing to do with Him!*

Yet during the entire time my mom battled with cancer, I never saw her express any anger at God or allow what was happening to take the smile off her face. Through chemo, sleepless nights, and days filled with pain, she was always quick to remind me that God is good no matter what. Because of her example, I learned that I could hold on to the promise that even when things don't look great, He can still be fully trusted.

My mom was always my biggest fan. I played football for a youth rec league and was absolutely horrible. It didn't matter—my mother was at every game.

But that was before she got sick. The next season, the doctors discovered the cancer shortly before football began, and she was too sick to attend any practices or games. I would get dressed for a game and come into the living room, where she would be sitting in her chair, to give her a kiss before I left.

The cancer was attacking her body with relentless intensity, and she was in constant pain. She probably weighed about one hundred pounds.

Near the end of the season, my mom got it in her mind that she would attend one of my games. I will never forget the resolve in her voice as she said to my dad, "I'm going to this football game."

My dad didn't argue. He picked her up, put her in the car, and set up a lounge chair for her at the field. She stayed for the whole game, and every time I made a play, I could hear her cheering.

Even when her body was failing her and she had no physical strength left, she refused to give up. She would not fail me.

My mom modeled that leaders don't allow circumstances to hold them back from what's important. She may not have won any awards for her leadership, but her legacy of never-failing love lives on.

* * *

Sometimes the best leadership advice comes from the most unexpected sources: from the life of a mother in South Carolina whose time was cut short too soon, or from the letter of an apostle, written some two thousand years ago.

Whatever your sphere of influence—whether you're managing a corporation or heading up a small group that meets in your home—I hope these leadership principles will sink into your heart and mind and daily habits.

Instead of approaching leadership the way the world does, with a hunger for power and self-advancement and competition, may you see that the best style of leadership is through love.

Love is patient, love is kind. It does not envy, it does not boast, it is not proud. It does not dishonor others, it is not self-seeking, it is not easily angered, it keeps no record of wrongs. Love does not delight in evil but rejoices with the truth. It always protects, always trusts, always hopes, always perseveres.

Love never fails.

1 CORINTHIANS 13:4-8

SUMMARY STATEMENTS

→ **Leadership isn't about the position you hold but rather the person you are.**

→ **Leaders don't allow circumstances to hold them back from what's important.**

#BestWayToLead

ACKNOWLEDGMENTS

Thank you, Lucretia, for being an amazingly supportive wife and for telling me you believed in me and you believed I was a great writer. That comment kept me in the game! You have taught me more about integrity and persistence than any leadership book I've ever read. I love you . . . and I always will.

Thank you, Charisse, for being the best little girl on the planet. I love you—always and forever, no matter what.

Thank you to our leadership team at NewSpring:

- Shane: You have taught me way more than I've taught you!
- Wilson: You believed in this thing from the beginning!
- Moorhead: Your dedication to getting things done has challenged me.
- Michael: The way you process has helped me see things in a much more effective way.
- Paul: There is no way I could do what you do—thanks for saying yes and for coming on board.
- Brad: I never have to wonder what you're thinking. Leading with you is easy because I know you won't hold back.

To a few others on staff:

- Erin: I couldn't do what I do if you didn't do what you do! Thanks for all you do behind the scenes to make things happen.
- Ricky: Thanks for saying yes and for coming here even though you didn't know what you would be doing. You are a *great* leader.
- Margie: There is no one on the planet like you and Danny! Honestly, y'all are two of the greatest people God ever created—and my life would be in disarray if it weren't for your family!
- Molly: I am so proud of you and the woman of God you are becoming.
- Allison: If you weren't passionate about organization, my life would be a wreck.
- Lauren: Your smile and attitude are contagious. Thank you for being such a bright light on our team—all of us are better because we get to serve with you!
- Sarah: You are priceless! Seriously, you have no idea. Your encouragement, your willingness to do whatever it takes, and your ability to make things happen make the world a better place.
- Suzanne: Thank you for allowing me to cause stress in your life. There is no one else I would want doing what you do.
- Annie: Every time I see you, my heart fills with joy because of who you are becoming and the way you allow Jesus to work though you.
- Madi: There is seriously *no one* like you. I'm honored that you work at NewSpring, and I'm more thankful for you

than you will ever know. Your potential is unlimited, and your heavenly Father is so proud of you.

- Amy B.: Your laugh, hard work, and conspiracy theories have made my life so much better.
- Keri: Thanks for the way you always smile, even when my ideas are dumb!
- Lee: Dude, I freakin' love you! I can't believe you have stayed with me for fifteen years!
- Elizabeth: If you ever say you're leaving NewSpring Church, you're going to have to take me with you.
- Howard: The way you work behind the scenes to encourage leaders is going to impact people in ways you will never see this side of eternity.
- Campus pastors: I wish I could list all of you by name, but that would force this book to be printed in two volumes. I love and value each one of you, and I'm more thankful for you than you could ever imagine.

And then just a few others:

- David King: Thank you for being the first community leader to ever believe in me. I will never forget our lunches together.
- Clayton King: You are one of the best friends I have ever had—and one of the most encouraging people on the planet!
- Steven Furtick: Thanks for your friendship and the fire you have for people. Your passion is contagious, man!
- Bill Rigsby: Thank you for not firing me during the six years I worked for you!

- John Maxwell: You have taught me more about leadership than anyone else on the planet!
- Andy Stanley: Thanks for taking my calls and for believing in me—and for all the leadership materials you have allowed me to steal from you.
- Craig Groeschel: Thanks for teaching me and for setting the tone when it comes to the church being generous with resources.
- Robert Morris: Thanks for shepherding me well and for caring enough to have hard conversations with me.
- Dave Ramsey: Thanks for your friendship and for showing the world that a leader can be real and still make a difference.
- Gary Snowzell: Your faith to do whatever the Lord asks you to do has impacted my life more than you will ever know.
- Lysa Terkeurst: I can't thank you enough for your encouraging text messages and phone calls, and your willingness to walk me through how to be a better writer. Believe it or not, this book would not have been written without your help! When I grow up, I want to write just like you!

MEETING JESUS

IF YOU ARE READING this section of the book, I want to say a huge thank you for having the courage to do so.

I should let you know up front that I'm not the smartest person in the world, and I don't have the answers to every question a skeptic may have about God. I just know that on May 27, 1990, I prayed to receive Jesus into my life and that every good thing that has happened to me since that day has been the result of my relationship with Him.

If you're interested in finding out how to begin a relationship with Jesus, here are some principles I often lead people through.

> Everyone has sinned; we all fall short of God's glorious standard.
>
> ROMANS 3:23, NLT

Every single one of us has sinned. All we need to do is turn on the news or look online to see the downward spiral in our society. People don't have to try hard to be evil—we're just naturally bent that way.

It's not just that the world has sinned and is going in a bad direction; I've sinned myself, and so have you. There are things we've done wrong that other people know about and some things that are secret, but either way, the result is that we fall way short of God's glorious standard—which is perfection.

I've been in ministry for more than twenty-five years, and I've never had anyone approach me and confess, "Pastor P., I'm really struggling with how perfect I am!"

All of us have messed up, which leads to some pretty steep consequences.

> The wages of sin is death, but the free gift of God
> is eternal life through Christ Jesus our Lord.
> ROMANS 6:23, NLT

A wage is something we earn. When I got my first job at Ryan's Steak House, minimum wage was $3.35 an hour. When it was time to get my first paycheck, I'd worked twenty hours, so I was expecting to get a check for $67. (Imagine my disappointment when I discovered this pesky thing called income tax and realized I wouldn't even gross $67!)

A gift, however, is something we receive. We don't work for it; we don't pay for half of it—all we have to do is accept it with gratitude.

This verse points out that the wage (what we earn) for sin (what we've done wrong) is death! Not just physical death, but spiritual death that results in a severing of our relationship with God now and a separation from Him for eternity.

But then comes the Good News: the free gift of God is eternal life through Jesus.

Not through becoming a better person.

Not through donating money to charity.

Not through going to church.

The free gift God offers is through Jesus. Salvation isn't something we work for; it's something we receive.

> God showed his great love for us by sending Christ to die
> for us while we were still sinners.
> ROMANS 5:8, NLT

I used to think I had to become a better person before I could become a Christian. *After all,* I reasoned, *Jesus wouldn't want anything to do with me in my current condition.*

Over time, however, I realized that no one cleans up so that they can take a bath, right? I've never met anyone who said, "I'm so dirty and sweaty—I need to clean up so I can get into the shower." That would be insane! The reason we step into the shower is to get clean.

The same is true on a spiritual level. Romans 5:8 tells us that God made the first move by sending Jesus to die for us and pay our penalty for sin while we were still sinners.

We don't have to clean up to come to Christ; we are made clean as the result of coming to Christ.

> If you openly declare that Jesus is Lord and believe in
> your heart that God raised him from the dead, you will
> be saved.
> ROMANS 10:9, NLT

Becoming a Christian is not merely an invitation to go to heaven when we die but also an invitation to follow Christ for the rest of our lives.

As we see in Romans 10:9, salvation is surrender. We must declare that Jesus is Lord, which is essentially saying, "Jesus, I'm completely giving my life to You. Whatever You say to start doing, I will start. Whatever You say to stop doing, I will stop."

Part of being a Christian is believing that God raised Jesus from the dead. I won't try to make this an apologetics book; however, I will unapologetically say that the Resurrection is what makes Christianity unlike any religion in the world. If Jesus would have said all that He said and then died, we would have benefited from His ideas, but they wouldn't have been enough to change the world.

However, Jesus didn't stay dead! He rose from the grave and is alive today. The way I see it, that's a compelling reason to believe His Word. I've never known of anyone who predicted their own death, burial, and resurrection—and then pulled it off.

Everyone who calls on the name of the LORD will be saved.

ROMANS 10:13, NLT

This verse has provided so much comfort and assurance for me.

When I was wrestling with whether I should ask Christ to be Lord of my life, I dealt with serious doubt for a while. After all, I'd done some really bad things in my past that I was pretty sure disqualified me from salvation. However, the word in this verse that stands out to me is *everyone*. Jesus has never turned away people who asked Him to save them.

After I asked Jesus into my life, I would still mess up, do things I knew I shouldn't do, say things I shouldn't say, and so on. When that happened, I would begin to doubt whether I was really a Christian.

Any time I questioned my salvation, I would go back to this verse and let it remind me that I'd called on the name of Jesus and that it was because of His work (not mine) that I belonged to Him.

Jesus knew every stupid, sinful, foolish, and self-centered

decision we would ever make, yet He still created us and put us on this planet and chose us to be His.

If you want to surrender your life to Christ, you can do that right now. (It's not an accident that you're reading this!)

The way we surrender our lives to Christ is typically through prayer. Below is a prayer you can pray in order to receive Christ. Let me be clear: this isn't a magic formula; it's just a heartfelt decision to surrender your life to Christ.

> Dear Jesus, I know I'm a sinner and I need your forgiveness. I believe You died on the cross for my sins and rose from the grave. Right now I confess that You are my Lord and the Leader of my life. Come into my life and take complete control of me. Show me how to live the rest of my life for You one day at a time. In Jesus' name, amen.[3]

---

3 If you just prayed to receive Christ, I would love to hear from you. Drop me an e-mail at pastor@newspring.cc, and I will send you some information on what you can do now that you've begun your journey with Jesus.

SUMMARY STATEMENTS

→ We don't have to clean up to come to Christ; we are made clean as the result of coming to Christ.

→ Jesus knew every stupid, sinful, foolish, and self-centered decision we would ever make, yet He still chose us to be His.

#BestWayToLead

ABOUT THE AUTHOR

PERRY NOBLE IS THE AUTHOR OF *Unleash!: Breaking Free from Normalcy* and *Overwhelmed: Winning the War against Worry*. He is the founding and senior pastor of NewSpring Church, which was rated #2 on the Outreach 100 America's Fastest-Growing Churches list in 2013. His primary responsibilities are being a servant to Jesus Christ; a husband to his wife, Lucretia; and a father to their daughter, Charisse. Perry is also passionate about seeing people meet Jesus, leading his church staff, and pouring himself into other church leaders on local and global levels. In 2015, Perry won the John C. Maxwell Leadership Award. You can find him online at www.perrynoble.com.

A GIFT FOR YOU!

To help you on your journey to the most excellent leadership,

we would love to offer you *The Most Excellent Way to Lead*

branded notebook for free, while supplies last.*

Visit mostexcellentwaytolead.com to order.

MostExcellentWaytoLead.com
#BestWaytoLead

3.5x5.5" • 48 pages • *$2 shipping & handling charge

to me. I will make you a light to the Gentiles, and you
ng my salvation to the ends of the earth" (Isaiah 49:6, NLT).
symbolism in this verse is amazing.

h had in mind that this message would be a light to the
nation, but God's vision was for this message to be a light
ntire world.

h had a limited view of what God wanted.

of the worst things we can do as leaders is subject the
we're responsible to lead to our small, safe ideas.

ieve God always wants more for us than we want for ourselves.

ieve He wants our churches to be full of people who are
ith life and hope and are contagious in the communities
olanted in.

ieve He wants more with your business or company.

ieve He wants more with your family.

God gets glory when a church or business or ministry
numbers; however, I would argue He gets as much (if not
lory when a person who is unashamed of their faith leans
m, seeks to grow, refuses to believe lies about themselves,
dreams big to fulfill the vision God has in store for them.
od is as big as the Bible says He is and He can do as much
ible says He can do, then why, when we're making our plans
m, would we make our plans small, safe, and predictable?
ieve one of the best questions a leader in any field can ask
when they experience success is "What now, Lord?"

n't think the One who literally walked through hell will lead
e and predictable places.

en He says, "Go," He has a plan—one that will prosper us,
n us; one that will give us hope and a future; one that will
to put our self-seeking tendencies aside and love God and
vay more than we love our own comfort.

Leaders set the tone. And if we want honesty and transparency
to dominate our culture, we have to be the ones not only to declare
those things as values in our organization but also to live them out.

ARE YOU TAKING RISKS OR PLAYING IT SAFE?

It was early 2007, and I had to make a leadership decision that,
at the time, was the biggest leadership challenge I'd faced in my
entire life.

Our church had been portable for around six years. Since we
rented a building on Sunday mornings, we had to set up every
Sunday around five in the morning and then pack everything back
into trucks and trailers at the end of the day.

Then, in February of 2006, we moved into a permanent facility.
We were excited to have a home base, and we thought we'd be able
to cruise for two or three years.

However, within eight months of the move, our attendance
doubled, going from four thousand each weekend to more than
eight thousand.

We suddenly had some important decisions to make.

We couldn't turn around and build a second building—we
didn't have the land or the cash.

We were already out of space in our children's area, as we'd
underestimated the square footage we'd need to accommodate the
kids who showed up every Sunday.

Our student ministry was growing so rapidly that every two or
three months, the middle school and high school students outgrew
any facility we rented for them to meet in.

We had a number of people coming each week from Greenville,
South Carolina (about thirty minutes away). That group said they
couldn't convince their unchurched friends to attend with them

in Anderson, but if there were a NewSpring campus in Greenville, they thought it would be successful.

So the leaders of our church began meeting to see if we could accomplish all these things at once: expanding our existing children's space, building a new student ministry center, and starting our first multisite campus in Greenville. The total price tag came to $20 million.

The first time I heard that dollar amount, my heart sank into my stomach. This would take work—a lot of work. We'd have to begin a capital campaign and try to raise the funds. I'd have to spend countless hours meeting with people and casting a compelling vision. Nothing like this had ever been attempted by any church in our area.

I was in over my head—and I knew it.

During the meeting when we had to make the final decision about whether we'd launch the $20-million initiative, I had to call a time-out and tell the other leaders around the table I needed to go home for the day because I just couldn't get clarity on what I was supposed to do.

When I walked into the house, Lucretia took one look at me and said, "What's wrong?"

I told her about everything I was wrestling with and explained the $20-million price tag. "I just don't know if this is even possible," I said.

Then she said something I'll never forget.

She reminded me about a move our church had wrestled through when we were about a year and a half old. We had to go from one location to another, and the total cost of the move was about $46,000.

The people in our church gave as sacrificially as they could,

and we raised around $26,000, but we still ___ move simply was not going to happen.

After much negotiating with banks and ___ crazy enough to loan a start-up church $2 ___ one, and one of the church leaders and I ___ saying that if the church couldn't pay, we w ___

Was I nervous? I didn't sleep for three w ___ I saw God do amazing things, and the $20,(___

With this in mind, Lucretia asked me ___ would you trust God for $20,000 but not tr ___ lion? Isn't He able to do it?"

Oh, snap!

At that moment, the switch flipped in m ___ the decision that we were going to move forw ___ that had been put before us.

As I look back on that incident now, I real ___ seeking attitude to creep into my thought pa ___ back from taking God-sized risks.

I liked the idea of not having to work as ha ___

I liked the idea of putting the organizatio ___ cruise control.

I liked the idea of "playing it safe" and er ___ calm in my life.

I wanted what was best for me—but not wl ___ people I was there to serve.

Haven't we all battled this desire to coast a ___ reach a stage in our leadership where we cease t ___ and instead concentrate on maintaining the stat ___

When this happens, we'd be wise to look at ___ Isaiah in this passage: "You will do more than ___

A WORD TO CHURCH LEADERS

I believe that the local church is one of the most difficult organizations to lead, since everything we do has to have a clear vision behind it. As a friend of mine says, church leaders are responsible for painting a picture that produces passion in people and moves them to action.

If you're a church leader, that doesn't mean you should settle for lesser dreams than the world; in fact, it means your dreams should be *greater*.

If Disney can get people excited about a mouse and Apple can get people excited about a watch, then why can't a church get people excited about a life-altering vision that God wants to breathe into them?

The church is the only establishment that has been around for the past two thousand years. In the span of those millennia, systems of government have ceased, nations have risen and fallen, and businesses have started and shut down, but the church has stood the test of time. And if Jesus waits another two thousand years before He returns, the church will still be standing.

When I talk to other church leaders, I try to challenge them to cast a huge vision and dream big dreams—and refuse to apologize for doing so.

However, we need to do so with the right motives. Self-seeking leadership causes setbacks in the corporate world, but when that happens within the church, it's absolutely destructive.

As we take another look at the story of Saul and David, we see a transition in Saul's life that, in my opinion, marked the beginning of the end of his leadership. At first, Saul's motivation was in the right place: "Saul built an altar to the Lord; it was the first of the altars he built to the Lord" (1 Samuel 14:35, NLT). In

Scripture, building an altar was an act of worship; it was a public declaration of the greatness of God and a person's dependence on Him for all things. Saul's altar to the Lord showed that the focus of his leadership and the motivations of his heart were in the right place.

Tragically, however, we see his perspective change: "Early the next morning Samuel went to find Saul. Someone told him, 'Saul went to the town of Carmel to set up a monument to himself; then he went on to Gilgal'" (1 Samuel 15:12, NLT).

In just one chapter, Saul went from building an altar to the Lord to building a monument to himself—and from this point on, insecurity, jealousy, and fear dominated his life.

It's awesome to want a growing ministry—after all, I believe God wants things to grow, and healthy things naturally grow.

However, we need to honestly ask ourselves, *Why do I want my church or ministry to increase in size and reach more people?*

If the reason is because you want to be recognized and given the accolades that come along with that recognition, then it's time to push the pause button and ask the Lord to change your heart.

Over and over again in my own leadership, I have to think through my own motivation, or I know my focus will veer toward "me" instead of "we."

Self-seeking leaders drop out of the race anytime it becomes challenging; however, leaders with hearts set on fire by God will have the strength and ability to push through any obstacle that comes their way.

I pastor a church made up of multiple campuses across the state of South Carolina. Our vision is that one day we will average 100,000 people at NewSpring campuses every Sunday.

It's an ambitious goal—one that has raised an eyebrow or two.

I've had people question me about having such a lofty goal, wondering if my motives are pure.

My only response is that I do what I do because I believe everyone's life would be better if Jesus were at the center. That vision motivates me every single day!

I remember what it was like not to know Christ—to live with no hope, no peace, and no assurance that something better was to come.

I remember what it was like to meet Christ and how He changed not only my eternal destination but also my earthly perspective.

I remember how Jesus changed the way I thought about things, the way I treated people, and the habits of my daily life.

I want every single person in the world to experience the kind of transformation I went through myself. In fact, if you've never made that decision and you want to know more about it, turn to the appendix on page 253.

As a leader, I've sometimes lost my focus and drifted into other reasons for doing what I do, but the Lord always brings me back, reminding me of where I came from. I do what I do in order to see more people transformed by Jesus' amazing power.

The following verse is my story:

> He reached down from heaven and rescued me;
>   he drew me out of deep waters.
>
> 2 SAMUEL 22:17, NLT

I want this to be the story for as many other people as possible.

If your vision is for people to meet Christ and have their lives changed by Him, and if that is the motivation of your heart, then make your plans big. Unapologetically ask people to get involved, because there isn't a greater cause on earth.

This kind of leadership is not self-seeking—in fact, it's others-focused, because the driving force behind it is the desire for people to become exactly who God has called them to be.

QUESTIONS TO HELP YOU LEAD IN THE MOST EXCELLENT WAY

Questions to Ask Yourself

1. What motivates me as a leader?
2. Do I have a purpose in life greater than my own achievement? If so, what is it? If not, how can I begin to cultivate that?

Questions to Ask Your Team

1. Does my leadership communicate that I care about your success?
2. What are two or three things I can do to better set you up for success?
3. Does my leadership seem to be grounded in myself or in a greater vision?

SUMMARY STATEMENTS

→ Self-seeking people don't seek God, because they don't want to share the credit for their successes with anyone.

→ Every leadership decision I've made that has produced any type of good fruit has been the result not of my brilliance but of God's goodness.

→ Time is one of the greatest leadership tools God ever created.

→ God most often develops our character when no one else is looking.

→ God always wants more for us than we want for ourselves.

#BestWayToLead

CHAPTER 9

NOT EASILY ANGERED

Love . . . is not easily angered.
1 CORINTHIANS 13:4-5

SEVERAL YEARS AGO, I went through an online battle that tore me apart inside. Some people were criticizing my character, my leadership, and my church, and it cut to some of the deepest places of hurt in me.

I wanted to engage.

I had some great one-liners to dish out in response.

I knew I could set those people straight.

However, I began to understand that arguing on the Internet is like peeing into the wind: it feels great at first, but it gets messy really quickly.

I'm pretty sure I'm not alone in this—every leader faces the temptation to get angry at some point in the course of leading their group or organization.

I could make this chapter really short and just say, "Don't be angry." However, I've found that it never works to tell people they shouldn't feel a certain way, because emotions are both unreliable and unpredictable.

Some people will try to send you on a guilt trip by telling you that anger is a sin, but that's simply not true. James the brother of Jesus said, "Understand this, my dear brothers and sisters: You must all be quick to listen, slow to speak, and slow to get angry" (James 1:19, NLT).

Notice he didn't say, "Don't be angry"; he said we must be slow to become angry.

In our desire to be excellent leaders, we will experience anger, but we can't let anger go unresolved. It's something that must be dealt with.

In his instructions on leadership, Paul says, "Love . . . is not easily angered" (1 Corinthians 13:4-5).

Anger should not be our default emotion.

If we throw things, yell, and call people names that would cause a sailor to blush, then we don't "have issues"; there's a deeper spiritual problem we need to deal with. And if you're feeling pretty smug because you've never had road rage or lost it with anyone on your team, don't skip this chapter. Quiet people can be controlled by their anger too, even if no one else knows about it.

When we allow anger to dominate the emotional landscape of our leadership, we create a culture of fear. People rarely flourish and live up to their potential in a fear-based environment; instead, they become paralyzed and isolated. Not only that, but this kind of environment eventually leads to a culture of dishonesty, because people are afraid of the consequences if they tell the truth.

DEALING WITH THE NAYSAYERS

As I've spoken all over the world and seen many different leadership styles, I've discovered that there's one area that causes nearly all leaders to become easily angered. It doesn't matter if they're male or female, in a church setting or a corporate environment, if they're a CEO or a mail-room worker—the one thing that can cause just about any leader to explode is one very particular group of people: critics.

If you've never dealt with critics, it's likely because you've never done anything significant.

The best way to completely avoid criticism is to embrace mediocrity with open arms and make up your mind to never try to be great at anything.

Criticism is nothing new for leaders, but because of social media, it's coming at leaders at a faster rate than any other generation has experienced.

That's why I believe some of the oldest advice about criticism is no longer relevant. You know, when someone says, "Criticism is like chewing gum: you should take the criticism, chew on it for a while, and then throw it away."

That might have been good advice a decade ago; however, it's not wise to follow that recommendation today.

Think about it—several years ago when people wanted to criticize someone, they had to sit down with a piece of paper and write a letter. Then they signed it (it was more difficult to be anonymous back then) and mailed it to the local newspaper. The newspaper would print the letter, and people would talk about it in barbershops and beauty parlors around town. Then, after about three or four days, it would go away.

Needless to say, that's not how communication works anymore.

Several years ago, a friend shared with me that because of the Internet, communication has these new characteristics:

1. Instant: We no longer have to wait a day or two to see what someone thinks about something; people's thoughts can be posted online in real time.

2. Constant: There's a steady stream of opinions related to any given subject all throughout the day (and night).

3. Global: While situations used to be isolated to a company or a community or a church, now people all over the world can see what's going on everywhere else.

4. Permanent: Once something is in the cyberworld, it's always out there, and it can be googled at any time.

If communication is instant, constant, global, and permanent, that means criticism is too. The chewing gum analogy breaks down in our context because there's no human being on the planet who can actually chew that much gum!

Whether you're a business leader, a pastor, or a stay-at-home mom, criticism has the potential to ignite a fire that consumes you and takes control of your emotions. And that's not because you're ungodly; it's just because you're a human being.

We need to figure out a way to deal with criticism, because it's the number one thing that can cause a leader to go from zero to blowing a gasket in 1.2 seconds.

It's not good for us as leaders to constantly be blowing a gasket because some guy on Twitter didn't like what we did or said.

Not only is it unhealthy for us, but it's also unhealthy for the team we lead. If people see us becoming obsessed and easily angered over what critics say, then they'll begin to operate the same way themselves. Before we know it, we'll be leading a rabid mob rather than a level-headed group of people committed to progress.

So how should a leader deal with criticism? We can't just isolate ourselves from everyone and shut down any form of feedback in our lives, or we'll let pride and arrogance dominate our decisions—and that's never a good solution (see chapter 6 if you need a refresher!). We need a healthy way to receive and learn from criticism.

For years I battled with anger whenever someone criticized me. I couldn't figure out a solution until a few years ago, when I became friends with Dabo Swinney, the head football coach for the Clemson Tigers. I began to attend some of his practices and watch the way he interacted with his players.

One day, after observing a really tough practice, I can remember getting into my car and having a revolutionary thought—one that has helped me get past my quick trigger for anger.

Thanks to Dabo, I know that if I'm going to accomplish anything significant as a leader and set a healthy pattern for my team, I need to begin to listen to my coaches, not my critics.

What are the differences between coaches and critics? Let me share seven of them.

Coaches Have a Relationship with You; Critics Hardly Know You at All

Mark this down: when we allow the voices of those who know us the least to shape us the most, we are in serious trouble.

Watching Clemson play football up close over the past several years has been awesome for me. I've been allowed to see the relationships that develop over time between the coaches and the players, and how trust is built in the context of those relationships. The players listen to the feedback the coaches offer, because of the extended time they've spent together and because the players know the coaches have their backs.

We've all been to sporting events where there was a loudmouth in the stands screaming his opinion to the coaches and the players. However, as often as I've witnessed that, I've never seen a player walk off the field and take advice from the person who most likely showed up at the game angry in the first place.

To the fan in the stands, the player is nothing more than a guy wearing a helmet and shoulder pads. But to the coach, the player is someone he has invested time and energy into.

I'm not a college athlete and I don't have coaches in the technical sense, but I've found that it's important for me to take a similar approach in dealing with criticism. If I'm going to receive criticism from someone, they need to meet the following requirements:

1. They must love Jesus.
2. They must love the church.
3. They must love me.

These requirements need to come in this order.

If the person loves me more than they love Jesus or the church, they won't tell me the truth, and they'll allow me to get away with things.

If they love Jesus and the church but don't love me, they might make assumptions about me that aren't true.

However, if they get this order right, I can trust that they're speaking out of a desire to correct, not condemn.

Coaches Assume the Best; Critics Assume the Worst

As leaders, why in the world would we allow someone who believes the worst about us to have control over us emotionally? This is not responsible leadership; it's insanity.

Whenever I've been corrected by the coaches in my life, they haven't approached me with the mind-set of "Perry is always screwing up and can never be trusted." Rather, their mentality is "Hey, man, I think you're better than this, so can you explain to me why . . . ?"

Critics are like savage wolves, waiting on an idea, quote, or strategic plan they can rip out of context and use to demonstrate to the world what a horrible person you are.

Critics rarely care about the people they criticize; they simply want to receive attention for their efforts. And when we allow them to consume our thoughts, we have ceased to lead and have begun to simply react.

Coaches know what their people are capable of, and they're willing to hold them to that standard—even when it's difficult or uncomfortable.

Coaches don't allow their people to underperform, because they want the best for them.

Coaches address the issues that come to the surface, but they do so while believing in their people, not dealing with them as failures.

Coaches Correct out of Love; Critics Correct out of Pride

Proverbs 27:6 says, "Wounds from a friend can be trusted."

Notice the Bible doesn't say, "Wounds from anyone who has an opinion about you can be trusted"; rather, it specifically refers to wounds from a friend.

One of the most frustrating scenarios when it comes to online criticism goes like this: a critic comes after you, and you don't listen to them or respond to them, hoping this will de-escalate the situation. But then your critic accuses you of being arrogant for not paying attention to them.

That accusation has always seemed ironic to me because it's more arrogant to "sit in the stands" and assume to know the game plan when you have no idea of the planning, preparation, and conversations that took place before the game.

When critics come after someone, their reason for doing so is usually not grounded in love. Their desire is not to see the person they're criticizing make a course correction and become a better person in the process. Most often, they want to see the person suffer, and they want to be recognized as the one who set them straight.

When critics confront, it's because they love themselves and want as much attention as possible. In contrast, when coaches correct, it's because they love the game and the players involved. They're acting out of encouragement, not anger.

Coaches Have Earned Respect; Critics Have Not

It's easy for us to say what the president of the United States should or should not have done, when none of us has actually served in the office of the presidency. We don't know the behind-the-scenes challenges the president faces or what deliberation has gone into a decision. The president has to make tough calls based not on what's popular but on what they believe is right.

You think our country has issues now; what if our president led by whatever was trending on Twitter that day?

In an ideal world, a president has advisers who care about the country and about them. The president trusts those people to say not just what's popular but what's true. If correction is to be effective, there has to be a level of respect established first.

Online critics often declare their list of achievements and then demand to be heard. However, if they had true credibility, they wouldn't have to spend so much time building a case for why they should be taken seriously.

Would you seek financial advice from the guy who has declared bankruptcy a couple of times?